PRAISE FOR
TAKING FLIGHT!
STUDENT EDITION

"*Taking Flight!* is an instant classic that will forever change how you see yourself and interact with others. The engaging fable that opens the book—and the enlightening discussion that follows—should be read by anyone seeking growth and success."

—**Ken Blanchard**, coauthor of *The One Minute Manager*

"This wonderful book contains the secrets to nurturing supportive and enduring relationships. *Taking Flight!* will enrich your life by guiding you to understand and celebrate differences."

—**John Gray**, author of *Men Are from Mars, Women Are from Venus*

"*Taking Flight!* is fun to read, but make no mistake—the lessons here are both practical and far reaching. This book is a real eye-opener."

—**Jon Housman**, CEO, Ora.tv

"As an educator, I found *Taking Flight!* to be a book that will teach students important principles for everyday life. I will make this book mandatory for my students."

—**Stan Kligman**, Clinical Professor of Marketing, Drexel University

"Rosenberg and Silvert write with humor, eloquence, and practicality—a rare combination. *Taking Flight!* got me looking at relationships from a whole new perspective."

—**Pam Levine**, Executive Vice President of Marketing, HBO

"This book should be read by teachers, parents, or anyone who wants to impact others in a meaningful way."

—**Michael Kozak**, Superintendent of Franklin Township Schools, New Jersey

"*Taking Flight!* offers incredible insight into why we say and do the things we do. We have applied this wisdom to our work team and have seen tremendous results. Definitely more than just another management book for your shelves."

—**Del Ross**, Vice President, Americas Sales & Marketing,
InterContinental Hotels Group

"This cleverly crafted fable demonstrates how the DISC system can break down the walls that too often separate co-workers. *Taking Flight!* is all you need to kick-start collaboration."

—**Frank Wander**, Chief Information Officer, Guardian Life Insurance Company

"*Taking Flight!* is destined to become the definitive work on the DISC styles."

—**Salvatore LoDico**, Vice President, Human Resources,
Agusta Aerospace Corporation

"*This* is the kind of book that changes corporate culture."

—**Lani Davis**, Manager, Human Resources, L-3 Tinsley

"Until now, there has been a void in literature that makes the concepts of DISC easily accessible. *Taking Flight!* fills that void. I will be making *Taking Flight!* a part of all my workshops."

—**Bart Puglisi**, Vice President, Talent Management, Penske Truck Leasing

"What a wonderfully insightful way to understand relationships. While there is terrific material in here for anyone in the corporate world, I find myself applying its lessons everywhere. *Taking Flight!* is a gem of a book and I will recommend it far and wide."

—**Monique Garret**, Head of Global Marketing, Octagon Research

"As an HR professional, I have been using the DISC styles for many years. *Taking Flight!* is a great vehicle for either introducing or re-enforcing this powerful model for understanding human behavior. The fable is fun and illuminates the styles in a clever way. The application section is packed with smart analysis and easy-to-apply DISC strategies. In a short number of pages, Rosenberg and Silvert have delivered both a highly readable and in-depth resource."

—**Marda Kornhaber**, Director of Human Resources, ITT

"Finally, an easy-to-read resource that millions of DISC users can reference to improve their relationship management skills. From the parable-like story that defines the major behavioral styles, to the concrete applications of DISC scores, *Taking Flight!* is packed with insights and easy to apply. Managers will want to keep copies handy for new employees, and consultants/trainers will find this a very useful tool for their clients."

—**Leonard S. Altamura**, former President/CEO,
Steininger Behavioral Care Services

"In *Taking Flight!*, authors Merrick Rosenberg and Dan Silvert have provided an insightful and entertaining allegory for today's often complex business environment. A modern business fable that guides managers to identify, understand, and blend individuals' characteristics and compatibilities into an effective team."

—**Gary M. Ilkka**, Vice President, Human Resources, Emerson Electric Co.

Taking Flight!

Master the DISC Styles to Transform Your Career, Your Relationships... Your Life

Student Edition

Merrick Rosenberg
Daniel Silvert

Vice President, Publisher: Tim Moore
Associate Publisher and Director of Marketing: Amy Neidlinger
Acquisitions Editor and Marketing Manager: Megan Graue
Editorial Assistant: Pamela Boland
Development Editor: Russ Hall
Operations Specialist: Jodi Kemper
Cover Designer: Chuti Prasertsith
Managing Editor: Kristy Hart
Senior Project Editor: Lori Lyons
Copy Editor: Chrissy White, Language Logistics, LLC
Proofreader: Sheri Cain
Interior Designer/Compositor: Gloria Schurick
Manufacturing Buyer: Dan Uhrig

© 2013 by Merrick Rosenberg and Daniel Silvert
Pearson Education, Inc.
Publishing as FT Press
Upper Saddle River, New Jersey 07458

FT Press offers excellent discounts on this book when ordered in quantity for bulk purchases or special sales. For more information, please contact U.S. Corporate and Government Sales, 1-800-382-3419, corpsales@pearsontechgroup.com. For sales outside the U.S., please contact International Sales at international@pearsoned.com.

Company and product names mentioned herein are the trademarks or registered trademarks of their respective owners.

Printed in the United States of America

First Printing: November 2012

ISBN-10: 0-13-334619-6
ISBN-13: 978-0-13-334619-0

Pearson Education LTD.
Pearson Education Australia PTY, Limited.
Pearson Education Singapore, Pte. Ltd.
Pearson Education Asia, Ltd.
Pearson Education Canada, Ltd.
Pearson Educación de Mexico, S.A. de C.V.
Pearson Education—Japan
Pearson Education Malaysia, Pte. Ltd.

Library of Congress Cataloging-in-Publication Data is on file and available upon request.

*Traci, your insight, support, and unconditional love
are the wind beneath my wings.
Gavin and Ben, thanks for being who you are.
—Merrick*

*For Cindy, your love and humor fill my life with joy.
For Eden, Benjamin, and Jakob.
—Daniel*

Contents

Introduction   1

PART I: TAKING FLIGHT! THE FABLE   5

Chapter 1   Home   7

Chapter 2   The Forest Grid   11

Chapter 3   The Council   15

Chapter 4   An Old Friend   25

Chapter 5   The Aftermath   35

Chapter 6   If a Tree Falls in the Forest...   39

Chapter 7   Reconnaissance   47

Chapter 8   The Four Styles   55

Chapter 9   Reflection   63

Chapter 10   The Awakening   71

Chapter 11   The Home Rule   77

Chapter 12   The Stakeout   93

Chapter 13   The Gathering   107

Epilogue   The Power of DISC   113

PART II: THE *DISC* MODEL   117

Go Online to Discover Your Style   120

The History and Mystery of the Four Styles   122

The Four Styles   123

People Reading   127

Seven Transformative *DISC* Principles   133

PART III: TAKING FLIGHT! *DISC* FOR COLLEGE STUDENTS   155

Paying for School   157

Dealing with Roommates   161

The School / Life Balancing Act   164

Choosing a Major   169

DISC and Your Teacher   173

Making the Grade with Group Projects   177

School Stress   180

Ace the Interview and Win the Job   185

Postscript   189

Appendix: Style Combinations   193

Acknowledgments

We are very lucky to have had many talented and caring people walk with us on our journey. Our co-workers at Team Builders Plus and Take Flight Learning—most notably, Jeff Backal, Ken Blackwell, Cathryn Plum, Stew Bolno, Aaren Perry, Andy Kraus, Lesley Cruz, Dolores Woodington, Heather Hafner, Andrea Bardon, and Britni Coleman—have been enormously supportive in helping this book take flight. To our parents, family, and friends, you have all contributed in ways you will never know.

Special thanks to Traci Rosenberg for her intuitive wisdom and to our talented editors, Cindy Silvert and Melissa Brandzel, whose owl-like clarity humbled a parrot and an eagle. We also want to thank Kulin Shah and the graphic artists at 3RDEYE for bringing the characters to life and to Todd Nordstrom for his insights.

Thank you to our publisher, Tim Moore and his team, for having the vision to put this book out there as only Pearson can. And last, thank you to Richard Andrews, whose passion and steadfast commitment successfully guided this book through every stage of the publishing journey.

About the Authors

Merrick Rosenberg, M.B.A., is an accomplished entrepreneur and keynote speaker. In 1991, he co-founded Team Builders Plus, the most recognized team-building company in the United States. Merrick has led team and leadership development training programs around the world for more than two decades. Drexel University honored Merrick as the Alumni Entrepreneur of the Year, and *NJ Biz* selected him as one of the New Jersey Executives of the Year. Under Merrick's leadership, Team Builders Plus was recognized as the New Jersey Business of the Year by *NJ Biz*, one of the Fastest Growing Companies in the U.S. by *Inc.* magazine, and on numerous occasions, as one of the Fastest Growing Companies and Best Places to Work in the Philadelphia region by the *Philadelphia Business Journal*.

Daniel Silvert, B.A., is a sought-after keynote speaker and executive coach. Daniel has led training programs at every level on the DISC styles, leadership, teamwork, accountability, and transformational change. Daniel's early background focused upon career development, coaching hundreds of executives through career transitions from both within and outside their organizations. Daniel has brought his unique perspective to hundreds of companies and government agencies, including Adidas, Blue Cross Blue Shield, Dell, Dow Jones, Home Depot, L'Oreal, L-3 Communications, Merck, SAP, Situs, W.L. Gore, and the Department of Homeland Security.

Take Flight Learning

Based on more than two decades of experience with the DISC styles, the authors co-founded Take Flight Learning to share DISC with the world. Take Flight Learning offers a variety of DISC training programs, products, and services. DISC sessions can be conducted for organizations (including programs for individuals, teams, leaders, salespeople, and educators), trainers (through the *Take Flight with DISC Certification*), and in public seminars. Merrick Rosenberg and Daniel Silvert are available as keynote speakers to enliven conferences with DISC wit and wisdom. And individuals can discover their strengths and challenges through the *Take Flight with DISC* profile.

Team Builders Plus

Team Builders Plus helps teams and leaders create more engaging and productive work environments. Team-building sessions range from team bonding events to facilitated interventions. On the lighter side, groups of just about any size can participate in treasure hunts, philanthropic activities, and an assortment of programs that are just plain fun. More intensive sessions are also available for groups who seek to build trust, improve communication, increase collaboration, break down silos, and instill accountability.

Learn more and connect with the authors:

ChiefParrot@TakeFlightLearning.com
(In case you're wondering, this is Merrick Rosenberg.)

TheEagle@TakeFlightLearning.com
(…and this is Daniel Silvert.)

Follow us Twitter at @DISCstyles, @MerrickR, and @DanielSilvert

www.TakeFlightLearning.com
856.807.0200

www.TeamBuildersPlus.com
856.596.4196

Like Take Flight Learning and Team Builders Plus on Facebook

Connect with the Taking Flight with DISC and Team Builders Plus LinkedIn groups

Introduction

Sometimes we discover a pattern so obvious and predictable that we can't believe we hadn't noticed it before. Imagine if this pattern could provide a blueprint for better understanding yourself and every person with whom you interact.

Such a framework exists through a simple four-style model of behavior known as *DISC*. The pattern is hidden in everything we do, and it might just be the most powerful tool you ever discover because it will enable you to maximize your potential and deepen your connection with everyone you know.

If you're already one of the millions of people familiar with the *DISC* behavioral styles, the principles shared in *Taking Flight!* will elevate your understanding to a whole new level. If you haven't yet been introduced to the four styles of *DISC*, brace yourself for impact: This knowledge will change your life!

In our work with hundreds of companies and tens of thousands of people from all walks of life, we have witnessed phenomenal transformations in people. We have watched mediocre managers evolve into highly effective leaders, teams mired in conflict resolve years of pent-up stress, floundering salespeople transform into superstars, frustrated teachers become inspirational educators, and countless careers revitalized and redirected by individuals who have learned how to fully leverage their natural gifts. As they replaced judgment with acceptance, couples have told us that understanding *DISC* saved their marriages, and parents have approached us with joy and relief at better understanding their children.

Whether you're interacting with coworkers or customers, family members or friends, *DISC* will empower you to better relate with others. You will soon understand why you click with some people and clank with others. Moreover, you will gain a valuable framework for maximizing your strengths and minimizing your weaknesses.

What you are about to read is not just a story about birds. At its heart, *Taking Flight!* is about *you*. Although you might not notice it at first, before long you will quickly recognize yourself in these pages. *Taking Flight!* is about why you react to your family, friends, and coworkers the way you do. It's also about how you respond to the world around you and what drives your decisions and actions. And, it's about how you can use this newfound knowledge in the future.

As you read, consider what *you* would do in the birds' situation and think about what that says about who *you* are, how you behave, and how your perceive and respond to the people in your life. Yes, this is just a story. But it's also a representation of your life. Believe it or not, you are one of the birds in this story. The question is, which one?

Is there a character in the story who acts like you?

Perhaps one of them reminds you of someone you know.

Do you find yourself cheering for one of the birds?

Do any of the characters push your buttons?

Birds know that in order to fly, they must first take a leap. They must jump from the secure branch that grounds them and head into the unknown that lies ahead.

If we wish to soar and reach new heights in our closest relationships, in our business careers, and in all aspects of our life, we too must take a leap. We all know that birds can *Take Flight*. The question is, can you?

PART I

Taking Flight!
The Fable

CHAPTER 1

Home

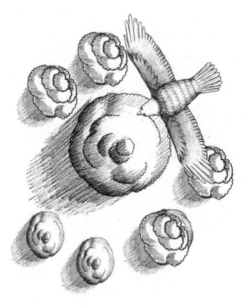

It began with a subtle crackling sound—hardly noticeable at first. Branches vibrated as the ground trembled below. Leaves shimmered. Suddenly, a booming snap echoed through the forest as the tree swayed one last time in the morning sun. Within seconds, the mighty tree would no longer provide shade for ground animals or shelter for birds. The two-hundred-foot giant hurtled downward, crashing to earth with a deafening thud.

An aftershock of anxiety rippled deep within the forest, known simply as "Home." To the diverse community of birds that dwelled there, Home was a place of safety and serenity. Here, fearsome eagles interacted with kind doves, and boisterous parrots mingled with watchful owls.

High above it all flew Dorian, a majestic eagle with a proud, sharp gaze and impressive seven-foot wingspan. From sunup to sundown, Dorian patrolled the skies. The mighty eagle felt a great sense of responsibility to ensure the security for all those who lived below. On this day, however, his sixth sense alerted him that something unusual had occurred. But what was it? Instinctively, his sharp eye and decisiveness kicked into a higher gear.

With focused attention, Dorian flew over a family of doves sharing quiet conversation. He noticed Samuel and Sarah sitting on their usual dependable branch preparing a meal for a friend. Their soft white and grey feathers blended seamlessly into their surroundings. Sarah was hatched in this tree, as was her mother, and her mother before her.

Typically, Dorian would hear soft cooing in sweet rhythmic tones as he glided past Samuel and Sarah's branch. The eagle never quite understood why so many birds went to the dove family tree to seek companionship, advice, and comfort.

But today, no cooing could be heard. The echoing thud had rattled the doves, and the resulting silence spoke volumes to Dorian.

The eagle continued his daily patrol and made certain to watch for Man or any other intruders. The birds enjoyed great harmony in their world, and Dorian intended to keep it that way.

He soared over the Great Lake and spotted a group of parrots. Though not large in number, they seemed to be *everywhere*. With a burst of red here and a flash of yellow there, parrot laughter reverberated from one end of the forest to the other. Dorian listened in for a few minutes as the parrots amused themselves with their usual banter.

"Hey everybody!" belted Indy, widely recognized as the forest's biggest personality. "Let's fly!"

"Where are we headed?" asked Ivy.

"We'll figure it out when we get there," Indy replied.

Passing just below, Dorian heard Indy remind the group, *"Life's no fun when there's work to be done. But we can make it better if we do it together. Yeah!"*

"That darn parrot motto. They are such time wasters," thought Dorian as he scanned the forest below. "Don't they realize that we need to figure this out right now?" If only they could just channel that parrot energy into something constructive."

CHAPTER 2

The Forest Grid

On the evening of the sound heard 'round the forest, owls Clark and Crystal were busy at work. Dorian flew by their nest and asked the owls if they could help find out what happened.

Clark waved Dorian away and said, "Can we talk later? We're almost finished with a project that may help assess the situation."

The owls were designing a forest map and grid that would enable Dorian to patrol the skies with maximum efficiency. Clark and Crystal had an innate ability to detect and analyze every detail of the world around them. This was coupled with an unrivaled knack for careful planning and organization.

Before they were ready to give the map to Dorian, they diligently employed their skills, checking and rechecking every last detail and working until the sky was orange with the morning sun. As Clark wrapped up his third and final accuracy check, he abruptly froze.

"What's wrong?" asked Crystal.

"This isn't right!"

"What is it?" she inquired. After all, their process had been rigorous, counting trees and meticulously recording every last variable.

"Well, I guess... we... it seems that... I can't believe I'm saying this, but our tree count is off," stammered Clark.

"How can that be?" asked Crystal. "Our count must be accurate if we're going to give this to Dorian."

They began to review their methodology when out of the blue—*bammmm, whapppp!* Parrots Indy and Ivy slammed right next to the owls and proclaimed, "The parrots have landed!"

Indy and Ivy laughed at each other. Clark rolled his eyes and thought, "Can't they see that we are *working?*"

"Good morning, Clark! Whatcha doin'?" asked Indy.

With a sigh of frustration, the owls reluctantly began to explain their project when Ivy interjected, "Details, schmetails. What's the big deal if you miss a tree? Whatever crazy stuff is going on out there will reveal itself sooner or later."

Baffled and stunned, Clark and Crystal stared in silence as the parrots continued to chat amongst themselves—swapping ideas about all the fresh and exciting ways they could spend their day. The owls just shook their heads and returned to the map. The parrots were a distraction, and the owls were anxious to present the eagle with a structured system. Surely *he* would appreciate their hard work and attention to detail.

CHAPTER 3

The Council

Dorian's frustration continued to build. The owl's diagram was not going to make a difference. The parrots' blind optimism wasn't going to solve anything. And this was certainly not a time for the doves to gather with close friends and family to comfort each other. The eagle wondered why he was the only bird concerned enough to take action.

The following morning, dark clouds hovered just above the treetops. Through the mist arose a piercing cry. It was Dorian, and, his screech meant only one thing; the eagle had found something. It was time for an emergency council meeting.

Many moons had passed since the last assembly of The Bird Council, and the entire forest was buzzing with apprehension.

All gatherings to discuss serious matters were held at the Council Tree, a massive redwood more than 200 years old. Almost as if it had been designed for meetings, the Council Tree featured two wide branches curved in a semicircle just underneath a protruding limb that served as a platform.

Because there hadn't been official business to conduct for a long period of time, the tree had remained empty—a symbol of the forest's serenity and security. That, of course, did not include the many secret, late-night, parrot-only comedy sessions, aptly named I-Team Improv, a tiny fact that Indy and Ivy chose not to share with Dorian.

The doves, represented by Samuel and Sarah, were the first to arrive at the Council Tree and settled into their usual spots. Their calm demeanor hid an underlying uneasiness, as they found it difficult to connect with their fellow birds in such a formal setting.

The doves warmly greeted Dorian, who was eager to get the meeting underway. The owls arrived next, ready to take detailed notes. All the birds waited in silence for the parrots—who could be heard chatting in the distance. Finally, Indy and Ivy strolled to their seats. "Give us the scoop, Big D," said Indy.

Dorian led all council meetings, just as generations of eagles had done before him. As usual, he cut to the chase: "We have a crisis on our wings."

A hush fell over the group.

"A large tree has fallen not half a mile from this very spot," the eagle continued.

"Oh, is that what this meeting is about? We saw that a few days ago," Ivy interjected. "It was right near the road, and there were some wolves hanging around. We were wondering..."

"You saw a fallen tree and didn't report it to me?" Dorian exclaimed, as he puffed his chest feathers. "Don't you understand? All of our nests are now at risk!"

Ivy shrugged. "We didn't think it was a big deal."

"A big deal? Do I have to remind you that we *live* in trees? What if this was *your* tree that crashed to the ground?"

"Relax," said Indy. "Trees have fallen before and I don't see why—"

"Not like this one," Dorian interrupted. "It was gigantic, healthy, and didn't just fall by itself. We need to get to the bottom of this. Now!"

"Maybe a big gust of wind knocked it down," proposed Ivy.

"Absolutely not!" screeched Clark, in a rare display of emotion. "Do you know the velocity at which such gusts would need to travel in order to do that? My estimate would be…." He began flipping through his journal. "Ah, yes, 86.7 miles per hour. Although, wind gusts of such magnitude are extremely rare. In fact, with a few calculations…"

"This was not a natural event," Dorian declared adamantly.

Sarah gasped as a wave of concern swept over her. Samuel comforted her. Silence fell over the group.

"Well?" Indy asked, nearly bursting with anticipation. "What was it then?"

"I don't know," Dorian said sharply. "But I'll find out."

The owls sifted through their notes. "We all need to stay calm and not jump to any conclusions before we gather the facts," said Crystal. She then turned to the parrots. "Let's review the situation. Indy and Ivy, you saw this a few days ago?"

"Yup," the parrots replied in stereo.

"I'm curious," Clark probed. "Why didn't you warn anyone using the Forest Alert System?"

"Didn't think anything of it," answered Ivy.

"Nobody pays attention to that anyway," added Indy.

"Why do we create these systems if nobody is going to use them?" muttered Clark.

"Now that's a good question," said Dorian.

Clark threw the eagle a dismissive look and returned back to Ivy, "So you saw the tree on the ground and just flew away?"

"Well actually, we were more interested in the wolves. Indy does this great impersonation of a howl. Do it Indy. You all have to see him…"

"Not now," Dorian snapped.

The doves, who still hadn't spoken a word, glanced nervously at the parrots and then back at the owls but did not enter the fray.

Clark, thinking he could offer a solution, waved his notes in the air. "Dorian, I'm wondering why you weren't flying along the new grid lines. It's quite efficient and might have allowed you to identify this situation earlier."

"Do you really think I spend my days following lines on an imaginary map?" snarled Dorian. "I don't think so."

Frustrated by the entire conversation, Clark stepped to the center of the platform. "My fellow Council members, we have developed processes and systems specifically designed to keep our forest orderly."

"Oh, come on," Ivy interrupted. The typically easy-going parrot was getting annoyed. "The purpose of Home is not to be *orderly*—it's to enjoy life. We shouldn't get worked up so easily. I say, 'Live in the moment, fly with abandon!' I still don't see what the big deal is here. Owls take the fun out of everything. I'm tired of it."

"That's all well and good for you and your parrot fantasy world," said Dorian. "But real life is not about playing games—though, if time permits, I see nothing wrong with healthy, competitive sports. Life is about accomplishments. We are here in this forest to leave our mark. Do you only want to be remembered for how much *fun* you had?"

Indy and Ivy shrugged and said, "What's wrong with that?"

"Everything is wrong with that!" exclaimed the owls.

Within a split second, the owls, parrots, and Dorian were all yelling at one another. Meanwhile, the doves continued to sit quietly in the background, alarmed that a full-blown conflict had broken out. Sarah squirmed uncomfortably.

"What should we do?" she whispered to Samuel. "The Council is coming apart. They're screaming at each other, and nobody is really listening."

Samuel tried to comfort her, but he was also upset. "We can't resolve anything by acting like this. We have to work together in harmony, or this situation will quickly turn into chaos."

Suddenly, Sarah had an idea. "I think we need some outside help."

"Xavier?" Samuel asked.

"The birds in the north are still talking about how he changed their lives after the big fire. It's worth a try."

"STOP!" screeched Dorian, his voice overpowering the owls and parrots.

Then Dorian turned to the doves. "Don't you two have anything to say? Or are you just going to sit there?"

Caught off guard and feeling pressured, Sarah stuttered to find words. She hadn't planned to speak and didn't want to sound critical, but now all eyes were on her. She took a deep, calming breath to steady her nerves. "Well, I can see everyone's perspective," she began warmly. "I agree with Clark's desire for order. We don't want to live in chaos. And I also see Dorian's point that one should seek to achieve important goals. As for what Ivy was saying, life ought to be enjoyed."

Everyone reluctantly nodded in agreement.

"And?" asked Dorian, already frustrated by her long response.

"I guess Samuel and I just want to live in a place where we can all be friends and feel safe," Sarah concluded.

"Is that it?" said the Eagle

His patience was exhausted. "With all due respect to your little pep talk, we've got a crisis here, and I'm going to figure out what's going on. I suggest that you do the same. If anyone observes anything suspicious, report back to me immediately."

The eagle leapt from his perch, and with a few mighty pumps of his wings he was gone. The group remained silent for a few moments, and then they parted ways. The Council meeting had, well, ruffled some feathers.

Although the birds had all lived in the same forest for many years, they had never faced a challenge like this before. Now, an uneasy mood hung over the land.

CHAPTER 4

An Old Friend

The next day, Samuel and Sarah rose early to journey to the northern tip of Home. Flying side by side, the doves passed over rolling hills and a towering waterfall. Following a creek that wrapped its way around mossy rocks, they noticed two humans gathering branches, presumably for a campfire. Gliding silently, Samuel and Sarah circled the red granite boulder where their trusted old friend Xavier could often be found. They almost missed him, as his chameleon skin blended seamlessly with stone.

Xavier was pleased to see the doves as Samuel and Sarah would rarely fly far from their comfortable nest. After a few minutes of exchanging pleasantries, Xavier asked, "Is there a reason for your visit?"

Samuel cleared his throat. "Actually, there is something we wanted to talk to you about."

Surprisingly, Xavier already knew about the fallen tree and had even heard about the heated tempers at the Council meeting.

"But how did you find out?" asked Sarah.

"News travels quickly," replied Xavier. "The Council meeting didn't sound particularly harmonious. And I assumed it would be the two of you who would seek advice."

"We don't know what to do," sighed Sarah. "Even the parrots are upset."

The chameleon grinned slightly. "Your kind once knew what to do, but over time, you have forgotten."

Puzzled, Samuel asked, "Doves knew what to do about falling trees?"

"No, no, no," replied Xavier. It's bigger than that. How do you suppose chameleons have managed to survive and thrive for so long? After all, most who live in this forest are seemingly far more powerful. And it's not about intelligence, although we have accumulated and passed down much wisdom over time."

Xavier paused. The doves looked at him blankly as the question lingered.

"The secret, my friends, is adaptability," Xavier answered.

The secret is adaptability.

"But we can't change our color like you can," said Sarah.

"True. But real adaptability is not related to appearance. It's much deeper than that. In fact, this knowledge is the key to the challenge before you...if you choose to accept it."

Intrigued, Samuel and Sarah asked Xavier to continue.

"Very well then," he added, "but I must remind you to be careful what you ask for. I cannot tell you what to do. I can only offer what I see."

With that, Xavier looked at them intently and declared, "You birds simply do not know each other."

Both doves cocked their heads. That didn't sound right.

Sarah hesitated, then spoke softly. "I don't mean any disrespect, Xavier, but we've known each other for generations. My mother was best friends with Crystal's mother."

Samuel chimed in, "And my father shared many stories of his experiences with both Dorian's father and grandfather."

"And when we were young," Sarah added, "we often played with Indy, Ivy, and the rest of the parrots. Of course, they were a bit wild for us, but it was never boring. I think we know each other quite well."

The chameleon smiled gently. "Allow me to clarify," he replied. "You have shared many experiences, but you do not truly *understand* each other, and this has prevented you from solving this crisis."

Xavier took a step toward the doves.

"Long ago, my chameleon ancestors learned that animals have four distinct styles of behavior. This understanding has been the key to our survival—and now, I'd like to share it with you. Let's look at your avian community."

Xavier picked up a small stick and drew an "X" on the ground. "I'm going to simplify this and instead of writing 'Dorian,' I'm just going to put the letter 'D' in the upper-left corner. At the upper right, he drew an "I" for Indy and Ivy. At the bottom right, he added an "S" for Samuel and Sarah and at the bottom left, he placed a "C" for Clark and Crystal.

The doves looked on as Xavier continued. Where was he going with this?

"Each of you has a distinct style, a certain way of expressing yourself and interpreting your world. If you truly understood how these four different styles behave, communication and cooperation would be easy. Unfortunately, you and your Bird Council members lack this awareness."

> *Each of you has a distinct style, a certain way of expressing yourself and interpreting your world. If you truly understood how these four different styles behave, communication and cooperation would be easy.*

Just then, the chameleon's body transformed into a stately golden brown.

"Wow!" Samuel exclaimed. "You look like Dorian!"

Xavier grinned. "Now think about what Dorian is like on the inside. He possesses dominant leadership skills such as decisiveness, vision, and an eagerness to take charge. He communicates directly and is extremely driven to achieve results."

"That's true," said Sarah. "I just wish he listened better."

"Dorian *is* a good listener, if one understands *how* he does so," Xavier explained. "Dorian does not listen with patience and empathy like you do. His style is to quickly assess the situation and offer solutions. That's not a poor listener; that's a problem solver."

"I never thought of it that way," said Samuel.

Just then, the chameleon's skin burst into a rainbow of purples, reds, greens, yellows, and blues. Samuel and Sarah laughed. They knew exactly who he looked like now.

"Like the colors that brighten their feathers," began Xavier, "the parrots add life to the forest. They display sunny optimism and live in the moment—which, for them, always seems to be filled with fun and excitement. They love interacting with groups and are quite effective at influencing others through their passion and enthusiasm."

"Yep, that's them," confirmed Samuel. "My mother always said that parrots could sell ice to penguins."

"Indeed," responded Xavier. "They also bring fresh ideas and creative solutions where others only see dead ends."

The chameleon's belly suddenly turned snowy white while his body transformed into a rich owl tan.

"Clark and Crystal, the owls, are in their element with small, often overlooked details. They instinctively analyze the world around them and reveal patterns about how things function and interconnect. Then they create systems to provide structure. Accuracy means everything to Clark and Crystal because without quality data, there is no solid basis from which to make sound decisions."

Sarah blushed and said, "I feel horrible. I always thought the owls were just being controlling by telling everyone how to do things."

"They may provide a framework, but they're trying to be helpful, not controlling," said Xavier.

Just then, the chameleon turned a gentle white and gray.

"Hey," Sarah laughed. "That's us!"

"You don't need to explain doves," said Samuel with uncharacteristic confidence. "We know ourselves."

"Ah, my friends, self-awareness is far more difficult to achieve than you might realize," Xavier sighed. "A great chameleon philosopher once said, 'To know oneself is the highest form of wisdom.'"

Samuel and Sarah looked at each other. How could they not understand themselves?

"Doves bring harmony and connection to your forest-mates. You care deeply about the happiness of others and listen with empathy and compassion. You are patient and calm, attracting others to confide in you when they are troubled. And although your steady energy is comfortable with gradual change, sudden disruptions that radically alter your environment are difficult for you to cope with."

"Like fallen trees?" asked Samuel with a laugh.

"Exactly!" confirmed Xavier, returning to his native shade of green.

"You really *do* know us!" exclaimed Sarah.

"This is a lot to digest," said Samuel. "I'm not even sure what it all means."

"What it means," Xavier replied, "is that there's a lot of room for misinterpreting one another. But with even this basic understanding of the four styles you can begin to appreciate the strengths and challenges of those who differ from you."

"I suppose that if all the birds understood the styles of others, we'd live in greater harmony," Samuel said, nodding in agreement.

"It would be wonderful to eliminate all this conflict," added Sarah.

The doves smiled, suddenly realizing that even the words they chose in their responses were in line with their newly identified style. They spent the rest of the afternoon with Xavier, delving deeper into discussion as night fell. Morning would bring a fresh perspective.

CHAPTER 5

The Aftermath

The next day, the entire parrot clan gathered together, feeling uncharacteristically upset about the Council meeting. Ivy felt that Dorian was being paranoid, and Indy didn't appreciate the eagle's dismissive tone. Clearly, things had gotten out of hand.

"We don't live in a 'fantasy world,'" Indy fumed to his fellow parrots. "This *is* reality. We look for the bright side because it's obviously there for anyone to see!"

"If the bright side isn't there," replied Ivy, "then how come we keep finding it?"

"Ya' got that right!" exclaimed Iggy, a senior member of the clan.

"Hey, remember when we got back from vacation last winter? Even the owls said it was quiet without us," recalled Iris, a young parrot in the crowd.

"Yeah," said Indy. "When we're gone, they miss the energy. But when we're here, they complain that we live in a fantasy world!"

All the parrots agreed.

Suddenly, Iris leapt off her branch and headed straight up to the clouds. Indy, Ivy, and Iggy followed right behind. All at once, they stopped flapping and dropped like rocks, screaming "Swaaaaaaaaaan diiiiiiiiiiiiiiiiiiiiive!" The bird that fell closest to the ground without crashing won the game.

They hadn't played Swan Dive for a while—not since the Ira incident—but today, it seemed necessary to lift the mood.

The familiar, happy shrieks reverberated throughout the land, delighting some and annoying others. "If one of those crazy parrots hits the ground again," thought Dorian, "I am *not* going to help this time!"

Not far off, Clark and Crystal each reflected privately on the day's events. Eventually, Crystal broke the silence.

"Clark, don't be upset about Dorian and the grid. He means well."

"I'm not upset," Clark stated.

"Really?" asked Crystal. "I would be if I were you."

"Well, I'm not," he reiterated.

After a few minutes of cleaning the same spot over and over again, Clark erupted. "You do realize that Dorian would have seen the problem immediately if he had followed our system. The fact that he just flies around up there admiring his 'big picture' without bothering to analyze what's happening down here in the real world is an outrage. And furthermore—"

"So, you're not upset?" Crystal interrupted.

"Of course not!" exclaimed Clark. "And don't get me started on those shrieking parrots."

"I understand," affirmed Crystal.

"Of course you do!" continued Clark. "They are completely oblivious to what is going on, and they have no sense of responsibility. Don't they understand the value of structure? They are so…*random*! How do they manage to feed themselves and keep their nests? It's inconceivable! The parrots have no respect for what owls contribute. Without us, this forest would be chaos."

"They seem to do just fine to me," smiled Crystal. "I'm just glad you're not upset."

"Me?" Clark insisted. "Not in the least."

CHAPTER 6

If a Tree Falls in the Forest…

Two days passed, and all was not well at Home. Tension hung like heavy fog. The sweet morning songs were muted, and most of the birds remained confined to their trees.

In the owl's tree, Clark and Crystal pored over the Council meeting minutes, intensely discussing various hypotheses and options. Meanwhile, the doves gathered in small groups but didn't discuss the fallen tree, as they didn't want to escalate the situation into a full-blown crisis. That wouldn't serve anyone.

The parrots, by contrast, remained hopeful and upbeat. They tried to deflect the increasing tension with humor, which only put the owls more on edge.

Dorian flew on patrol like a bird on a mission, resentful that nobody else shared his sense of urgency. At the same time, however, he was happy to be in command. And though he would never admit it, the heightened state of alertness made him feel more alive than ever. His intense focus and determination reassured the doves. Even Clark appreciated Dorian's resolve, though he still wished he had followed the grid.

Still, the eagle had little desire to engage in the drama of the crisis with the others. He chose to rise above it all and view the situation from 10,000 feet.

On Dorian's fourth pass of the forest, something caught his eye—an open space in a densely populated area where a tree had certainly stood. The eagle banked hard to the right and then lowered to an altitude just above the canopy. What he saw next sent his adrenaline soaring.

A large, mature elm with broad limbs and a sturdy base lay flat along the north bank of the Great Lake. Dorian's heart beat wildly as he swooped closer and spotted a second tree that had also been ripped from its foundation.

Immediately the eagle took action, bolting back toward the forest and releasing a booming screech that bellowed above the tree tops.

"Trees down!" he shouted to the parrots, who were weaving in and out of a nearby grove of hemlocks. "Two more trees are down!"

Dorian then landed, perched high atop the tallest oak as parrots swooped in from every direction, surrounding the eagle in a rainbow of curiosity.

"Two more have fallen. I cannot overstate the magnitude of this situation," he declared. "We've all seen dead trees collapse and live ones fall from lightning strikes, but these events are clearly different. Our number one priority now is to determine why this is happening and to stop it from happening again."

Delivering bullet-like directives, Dorian instructed the parrots to immediately gather forensic data from the crime scene and concluded with a brisk, "Any questions?"

Without a word from anyone, the eagle offered a quick nod and soared away. The parrots flew off in unison to what was now known as Crash Site 2.

Minutes later, the eagle passed over the Great Lake, landing with a thump and startling the owls from their sleep.

"Clark. Crystal. Gather the rest of your clan," Dorian commanded. "I need to speak with them, now."

Unaccustomed to being roused under a hot sun, the owls slowly lifted their sleepy heads while the eagle impatiently tapped his toe.

When they were awake, Dorian updated the situation and directed the owls to fan out and interview as many creatures as possible. "See if anyone heard or saw anything," he instructed. "If they did, report directly back to me immediately."

"What would you like us to ask them?" inquired Crystal.

Crouching down for take off the eagle retorted, "Find out what they know."

"What if—?" Clark began to ask, but the eagle was already gone.

As he rose above the forest, Dorian did not hear the same flurry of activity that followed his parrot tree departure. Glancing back at the owl tree, he watched in horror as they gathered in a circle with pens and paper. "What the—?" Dorian made an abrupt U-turn. Again, he landed in the owl tree with a thump and startled the owls, "This is not the time for taking notes! You need to get going *now*. Conduct interviews and report back to me."

Departing again, he thought, "They have no sense of urgency. I don't know how they get anything done."

None of the owls liked how Dorian had spoken to them.

"Who does he think he is?" thought Clark. "What gives him the right to boss us around? He doesn't understand that our systems enable the results that he supposedly cares so much about. As my father always said, 'Aim twice, strike once.'"

With a dismissive look at the eagle in the sky, a defiant Clark declared, "Let's do this *right*."

Meanwhile, on the other side of the Great Lake, Indy, Ivy, and some parrot friends arrived at Crash Site 2. As they approached the scene, they spotted a pack of wolves splashing in the water and then fleeing along The Road.

The parrots gazed at the fallen trees.

"These are whoppers," marveled Indy. "Look at the size of them!"

"Were there any nests?" asked Ivy.

"Just one, but it looks like it was abandoned a while ago, so no real harm was done," Indy replied happily. "So what are we looking for anyway?"

"Clues!" shouted Ivy. "We're detectives now."

"That's awesome," agreed Indy, then cocking his head. "Hey, why are there wood chips everywhere?"

"Well," said Ivy, "this *is* a forest. Wood should be everywhere."

"You know," Indy realized, "if we solve this mystery, we'll be heroes!"

"Right," nodded Ivy, "They'll throw a parade in our honor. We'll go down in history."

"Imagine what the owls and eagles will think of us then," added Indy. "They'll realize there's more to us than just having fun."

"And after the parade," said Ivy, "we could establish a holiday to celebrate our discovery."

"Totally," agreed Indy.

Then, just a few feet away, Indy spotted something that looked like an old piece of red cloth.

"Check this out," he said. "I think it's a clue. Man is the only species that could have left this here. I think it's called litter," Indy smirked giving Ivy a playful nudge.

But Ivy wasn't paying attention. She was busy pointing to the ground with a quizzical expression. "The branches are missing."

"That is actually weird," agreed Indy. "But, it's hardly newsworthy enough to track down Dorian. It's getting dark. Let's head back and get a fresh start in the morning."

And with that, the parrots took off in a flurry of color.

Meanwhile, the owls were still busy crafting perfectly worded interview questions.

C H A P T E R 7

Reconnaissance

Two days later, everyone convened at the Council Tree to report their findings. Clark fixed his eyes on the parrot representatives. "Indy and Ivy, what did you find out?"

"Let me tell you," replied Indy excitedly. "We got tons of information!"

"Loads of good stuff," added Ivy. "For starters, we saw a pack of wolves at the scene."

"I don't think wolves took down a tree," noted Dorian dismissively. "What else did you get?"

"Well, the branches were gone," said Indy.

"Gone?" asked Crystal.

"Where did they go?" asked Dorian.

"They didn't *go* anywhere," Ivy responded. "They were just gone."

"Were there any marks on the stumps where the branches had been?" probed Clark. "Did you inspect the area to ascertain what might have happened to them?"

Ivy looked at Indy. Indy looked at Ivy. An uncomfortable silence settled over the Council.

"Look," Indy said defensively, "it had just rained so the ground was all muddy. There wasn't really anything to look at other than wood chips scattered around. The branches were just gone."

Clark frowned. "That's it? That's what you call a 'ton of information?' Did you assess the splatter pattern of the chips? Did you draw a diagram of the scene for us to review?"

Ivy looked at Indy. Indy looked at Ivy.

Clark shook his head in disbelief.

Dorian scowled and said, "Okay. Let's move on. Clark, what did you and Crystal find out?"

"Well, unlike the self-proclaimed 'I-Team' of Indy and Ivy, we streamlined our interviewing efforts to those creatures who were in a position to know what had actually transpired. Crystal and I set out at 6:00 a.m. sharp yesterday for Crash Site 2. We immediately identified seven potential creatures to interrogate: two amphibians—a frog and a salamander; two reptiles—a snake and a turtle; and three mammals—a chipmunk, a groundhog, and a mountain lion. The order in which we approached our potential witnesses required an analysis of their daily routines so that we could—"

"Seven?" whispered Indy to Ivy. "We would have spoken to fifty."

As Clark continued with a detailed description of their preparation activities, Dorian stared at the owl with his eyes open wide.

"He must be impressed," thought Crystal.

"You *cannot* be serious!" the eagle erupted.

"You don't like the plan?" inquired Clark.

"The plan?" snarled Dorian incredulously. "I don't even like the *idea* of the plan!"

"Obviously," a resolute Clark explained, "you are incapable of comprehending the meticulous care that we have employed to determine the most logical course of action—"

"Okay," Dorian interrupted. "So what did you learn?"

Clark sighed. "I'm getting to that. As I was saying, we created an interview schedule that allowed us to acquire information regarding—"

"*What* did you learn?" repeated a now-thoroughly agitated Dorian.

"Well, the interviews were not as fruitful as we had anticipated," conceded Crystal.

"Did you discover *anything*?" bellowed Dorian.

"Well, nothing yet, but..."

Dorian raised his wings in defeat as Indy and Ivy smugly grinned.

"Nobody had the capacity to tell us anything of value," continued Clark. "But it should be noted that we now have a process that will allow us to efficiently gather information should there be another occurrence of—"

Indy jumped in. "Come on, Clark. You must have learned *something*."

"Well...um...the chipmunk seemed particularly suspicious," noted Clark. "As soon as we began our questioning, he immediately fled up the nearest tree!"

"He ran away?" inquired Ivy. "Chipmunks are some of the friendliest animals in the forest. How did you approach him?"

"After careful consideration, I opened with, 'Where were you yesterday at precisely 10:15 a.m., and what were you doing?'"

"I guess that's owl-speak for 'How are ya'?'" Indy smirked.

"Wow," added Ivy. "I'll bet the other creatures couldn't wait to hang out with you, either—while you interrogated them!"

"We weren't there to 'hang out,'" Clark responded calmly. "And at least *I* would know how to assess crime scene evidence that was clearly plain as day. What were you actually doing there? Imagining your victory parade?"

Indy looked at Ivy. Ivy looked at Indy.

Dorian was beside himself. "This is unacceptable. None of you obtained any usable intelligence!"

"Okay, what did *you* find out, Mr. Big Shot Eagle?" snapped Ivy.

In a rare alliance with the parrots, Clark chimed in, "Indeed, O' Great One. Tell us what your random 10,000-foot flyovers have revealed. We're all ears!"

Dorian was seething. "Were it not for me," he declared, "none of you would even have a clue about what's happening here! You'd all be sitting around waiting for the next thundering crash."

"Really," snapped Clark. "Who put you in charge, anyway?"

"That's enough," interrupted Samuel in a firm tone.

Stunned, the other birds turned to him. The dove didn't speak up often, so when he did, it got everyone's attention.

"Sarah and I invited a friend, and we'd like you to hear what he has to say."

The Four Styles

Threeee Council members watched the sky in anticipation. They were curious to meet Samuel and Sarah's friend. They were startled when a voice came from the tree itself.

"Thank you for having me," said the voice, as if a branch had come alive. "It's an honor to meet all of you."

Sitting beside Sarah was the chameleon, Xavier.

The Council members stared in disbelief as Clark proclaimed, "Non-avian creatures are strictly prohibited from Council meetings unless approved of by a two-thirds majority vote."

"We're sorry, Clark," explained Sarah, "but given everyone's sensitivity over the crisis, we felt that we needed some outside support."

"Bold move," thought Dorian, impressed by the doves' initiative. "Maybe *he* knows something."

The chameleon scurried up to the podium and silently examined the assemblage before him. The birds wondered what he was thinking. After what seemed like a very long pause, Xavier finally spoke. "So many colors to choose from," he marveled. "What great diversity in this group. Imagine if you all appreciated it."

"Right now there's not much to appreciate," mumbled Dorian.

The chameleon crawled down from the podium and beckoned the birds to form a small circle around him. The eagle and owls found it awkward being so close to the others but grudgingly complied. Samuel and Sarah felt right at home. They loved nesting like this.

With the full attention of the birds, Xavier explained the four different styles: the eagle's decisiveness, the parrot's enthusiasm, the compassion of the doves, and the accuracy of the owls. The chameleon then took a step back and sat quietly.

> *Xavier explained the four different styles: the eagle's decisiveness, the parrot's enthusiasm, the compassion of the doves, and the accuracy of the owls.*

"So," Clark asked, "what does this mean for us?"

The chameleon slowly turned his gaze from one Council member to the other, transforming into a dazzling collage of colors representing all of the birds. The doves smiled at each other.

"Sure," said Ivy, "that's easy for you to do, you're a chameleon!"

"Actually," replied Xavier, "it's not a simple feat to assume the color of those around you."

This surprised the birds, who knew little about other species.

"For me to display your color, I must understand you," he explained. "When I look at Dorian, I feel his confidence and authority. This understanding allows me to assume his appearance. When I look at the parrots, I embody excitement and freedom. Suddenly, life is full of opportunity and optimism. With the owls, I sense precision and order. I experience a structured world that ensures quality and accuracy. And when I connect to the doves, I feel harmony and compassion. I experience a sincere caring for the well-being and happiness of others."

The doves tingled with satisfaction. For the first time since the initial tree fell, they felt the group was coming together.

Suddenly Dorian snapped, "Are you suggesting that I should *hang out* with the parrots just for kicks and complicate anything and everything to better understand the owls? I can't do that. I'd be neglecting my leadership responsibilities, not to mention wasting my time!"

"Oh *paa-leeeeease*," interjected Indy. "What has all your *leadership* actually amounted to?"

Samuel and Sarah sighed in disappointment.

Clark studied the chameleon carefully. "I must say that while I find the four styles fascinating, I have no intention of abandoning logic and analysis in favor of these other…ahem…qualities you have described in the others."

Sarah was upset. She had worked hard to unite the group, and it took a lot for her to stand up to the Council, but this had gone too far. "Everyone, please," she pleaded. "Don't you see? This—how you're all behaving right now—is exactly what Xavier is talking about."

Xavier nodded calmly. "You are all so caught up in your own worlds that you think that *your* way of doing things is the *only* way."

> *You are all so caught up in your own worlds that you think that your way of doing things is the only way.*

"What's wrong with that? My way works for me. And it worked for my father before me and his father before him," stated Dorian proudly.

"Same here," the parrots agreed in unison.

"Well," the chameleon said, "I'm glad you're all in agreement about *something*. But, if you wish to solve this crisis, you need to be more accepting and less judgmental."

Clark folded his wings across his chest. "This is a lot to absorb."

"I still don't think you all respect what I do for this place," said Dorian.

"I'm not convinced that you appreciate me and the other parrots," said Indy.

Xavier's color returned to a wooden shade of brown. Samuel nodded at his friend feeling defeated. "Thank you. My apologies that you came all the way here for…"

Xavier nodded back at Samuel. Then, the chameleon slipped away as the other birds continued to bicker.

Samuel and Sarah glanced at each other as the volume of the squabble continued to escalate.

"Is this how it's going to be now?" Sarah wondered.

Before the trees had begun falling, the forest had been such a peaceful place. And although the birds knew that they were all distinct from one another, they had assumed they shared more similarities than differences. Now they weren't so sure.

It was a cold night at Home.

CHAPTER 9

Reflection

The birds spent the next day with those of like feathers. The parrots commiserated about the negativity at the Council meeting. There was too much dwelling on the past rather than envisioning a hopeful future.

Clark and Crystal organized an owls-only meeting to review Xavier's theories and discuss their efficacy. Had other owls observed the four styles as well? Was their experience consistent with his model? There was much analysis and debate.

Samuel and Sarah invited a few dove friends over for a light snack. The group voiced discomfort about the lack of harmony in the woods. They now feared that Xavier's insights might have driven everyone further apart instead of bringing them closer together.

As Dorian surveyed Home from above, he flew with a renewed sense of purpose. He had to prevent another tree from falling.

While thinking about the previous day's debate, he still felt that his efforts weren't properly respected by the others. Yet, after crisscrossing above the land for a while, Dorian began to wonder if he was, in fact, judging others as Xavier had described. If so, then as the leader he could very well be a big part of the problem, and that would be unacceptable.

Dorian's action-oriented style didn't often lend itself to deep reflection. However, if he were truly part of the problem, then he needed to fix it immediately.

Then it hit him.

"What am I doing?" he said aloud. "We can solve this now."

As the sun began to set, the eagle flew over the treetops where the parrots congregated. He circled twice to gather his thoughts.

All the parrots looked up. They were surprised to see the eagle so soon after the Council meeting blowup.

Dorian landed. He cleared his throat. And, then, he smiled. What followed was something extraordinary. The eagle approached a few parrots he didn't know well and made awkward attempts at small talk. The parrots didn't know what to make of it—Dorian had never done this before—but they welcomed him anyway. Then, after a few strange pleasantries, Dorian approached Indy and Ivy and cut to the chase: "We need to fix this situation between us so we can solve the real problem at hand."

The parrots all nodded as Ivy responded, "We couldn't agree more. We don't like all the sniping. It's getting us nowhere."

Dorian paused for a moment. The eagle was about to eat a slice of humble pie, and he wasn't sure if he could swallow it.

"I realized something earlier today. That little lizard may be right. I haven't acknowledged how valuable parrot energy and optimism is to all of us. You obviously play an important role."

For once, the parrots were speechless.

Dorian continued. "Remember when that freak windstorm hit a few years back?"

"Oh yeah. That *was* freaky," said Indy. "It came out of nowhere!"

"Yes, it did," said Dorian. "That swirling funnel ripped through the forest so fast that we barely had time to react. It was you—all the parrots—that were creative and immediately found a solution. Your idea to fly high above the clouds kept us safe until the storm passed. You guys are real innovative thinkers."

The parrots proudly puffed up their chests as they relived the episode. They had, after all, risen to the occasion on that one.

"So," concluded Dorian, "I haven't tapped into your talent for fresh ideas. Instead, I've been expecting you to act more like me...and that's crazy. In fact, if everyone were like me, then we'd really have a problem."

With that admission, they all laughed.

Then Ivy volunteered, "I've been thinking about what Xavier said, too—about expectations. I guess I expect others to react to situations like I would."

"I know exactly what you mean," Dorian acknowledged. "I get frustrated when others can't do what I can do."

"Yeah," said Indy. We often don't understand why other birds don't enjoy the same things we do."

"And, when they don't meet our expectations, we judge them for it," said Ivy.

Dorian thought that there really was more to these parrots than meets the eye.

Then he added, "So, it was unrealistic to expect you to respond to things as I would, and vice versa. Truth be told, facing challenges and solving problems energizes me."

"That's because you're good at it, Dorian," affirmed Ivy.

The eagle grinned. "I guess we all need to get smarter about what each of us brings to the forest. Then we'll be able to solve this crisis. *Any* crisis."

At that moment, the sun disappeared beneath the horizon, and the parrots announced in unison, "Happy Hour!"

"Seems like it's always 'Happy Hour' for you guys," joked Dorian.

"I think it's time," said Ivy, playfully nudging the eagle. "You're coming with us."

Dorian chuckled, suddenly feeling game. "Sure, why not? So what happens during Happy Hour?"

"Oh, you'll find out," smirked Indy.

CHAPTER 10

The Awakening

The following night, Sarah was startled by a cracking sound. While dozing back to sleep, a loud snap jolted both her and Samuel awake. Their nest slid left, careened right, and then shook violently.

"We need to leave now!" screamed an alarmed Samuel.

"Wake everyone on the east branches! I'll head to the west side!" cried Sarah.

As the two doves sped from branch to branch, the forceful shaking had already woken a number of doves, but most were too groggy to understand what was happening.

"We need to go!" shouted Sarah.

"What?" responded one of Sarah's cousins, "I can't just pick up and leave."

"You can and you will!" Sarah commanded, startled by the force of her own words.

The entire tree rocked left, and a thick branch crashed onto a nest, trapping two birds and their chicks inside.

"Are you okay?" Samuel called.

"We can't get out!" the birds squealed.

Samuel spotted a group of doves escaping from their nests and called out to them. "You two!" he said pointing to the other doves. "Get on that side of the branch. The rest of you, over there!"

Frazzled and shell-shocked at having to escape from their nest only to be called back to the tree, the doves just flew in place—frozen in mid-air.

"Now!" commanded Samuel. "On the count of three, you're going to lift the branch and I'm going to pull them out. One, two…"

Just then, the tree rocked violently to the right and the nest began to slide. The branch that had trapped the family of doves inside was now the only thing holding the nest in place.

"Can your chicks fly yet?" shouted Samuel.

"No!" the parents responded. "We can't carry them all! What are we going to do?"

Sarah arrived just in time to see the situation. The sound of wood splitting and branches snapping was growing louder.

"We can carry the nest!" she shouted as she signaled to a group of doves to join her. "You four lift the branch up, and you three get underneath. We're going to catch the nest as it slides down and carry it on our backs to the ground!"

"What?" the other doves exclaimed in shock. "We can't! We've never done that before!"

"Well, you're going to do it now," declared Samuel, smiling proudly at Sarah.

The tree violently jerked backward. The first group used the momentum to lift up the branch. The nest immediately slid down, and the family grasped their chicks. The tree leaned further away, and the nest seemed to magically level out in the air. The dove family had no idea what how it was working, but it was working! With Samuel and Sarah now joined by numerous other doves underneath, they gently lowered the nest to the ground. A moment later, an enormous crack erupted, and the doves' beloved tree slammed into the creek below with a thunderous splash.

The doves huddled together at the base of their fallen tree. Wood chips littered the ground, and Samuel noticed a strange set of fresh footprints that led away from the scene.

Sarah sat down to regain her composure. Beyond the stress of losing her home, she had never taken charge in a crisis like this before and needed to catch her breath.

The rest of the doves remained quiet, staring in disbelief.

A short time later, the doves flew off to seek a safe place to rest. The parrots had been awakened by commotion and immediately took the doves in for the night. Ivy and Indy sat stunned as Samuel and Sarah recounted the night's horrible events.

"Now it's personal! We're going to find out who did this," vowed Indy.

Ivy looked at Samuel and Sarah with newfound respect. "You guys are heroes!" she proclaimed.

Both doves blushed.

"I will say," conceded Sarah, "I felt a bit like Dorian out there, ordering others around and making things happen."

"Yes," chuckled Samuel, "you did a fine eagle impersonation. I never realized how useful a little decisiveness could be."

CHAPTER 11

The Home Rule

Within hours, all of Home was buzzing. An emergency Council meeting was called for dawn the next morning. The Council members arrived just before sunup, except for Samuel and Sarah, who were scouting new trees to inhabit.

The parrots were fueled with passion. "Nobody does that to our friends and gets away with it!" declared Indy.

Clark added, "We've got to get it right this time. There is no margin for error."

Dorian stepped up to the podium. He had more bad news for the Council, and there was no time to waste. "Three more trees went down last night at the northern tip of the Great Lake. Dozens of nests were destroyed. Fortunately, everyone got out in time."

"Three more!" Ivy exclaimed, clutching her chest with anger.

"This situation is escalating out of control," Clark stated flatly.

"Listen," Dorian declared, "it's up to all of us to solve this crisis. There's no more time for bickering." He stood tall, adding, "I take full responsibility for how our last meeting ended. My words weren't helpful to achieving our objective, and I vow to do better this time."

The Council members, floored by the eagle's uncharacteristic humility, nodded in appreciation.

"In fairness, most of us weren't open to what Xavier had to say," Clark added. "And we certainly were oblivious to the value each of us contributes to the forest."

Dorian replied, "You're right, Clark. I've been thinking about how we handled the last crash site, and I want to try something different this time."

"Let's go for it," said Indy.

"After the two trees fell the other day, I delegated responsibilities without being aware of our different styles. This time, each of us will focus on what we do best."

"Excellent," stated Clark, "and if I may say so, right now your decisiveness is what we need in a leader."

"Thank you, Clark. We're going to figure this out," continued Dorian. "This time, the parrots should interview potential witnesses to find out what they know. Indy and Ivy will have everyone relaxed and talking to them in no time at all. Heck, they know everybody."

The parrots beamed.

Turning to Clark and Crystal, Dorian resumed. "You should investigate Crash Site 3. I know your Owl skills will gather useful data for us to evaluate."

"Consider it done," Clark said, energized for action.

"Excellent," affirmed Dorian. "Let's meet back here at sunset to review what we've learned."

The birds dispersed and worked diligently throughout the day. The parrots conducted one interview after another as the owls took pages of crash site notes. Promptly at sunset, the birds reassembled at the Council Tree, including the doves, who had already chosen a new family tree.

Before the meeting began, Samuel and Sarah thanked everyone for their support.

Clark shook his head. "Honestly, you doves always put the needs of others before your own. Of all the birds in the forest, I can't believe this would happen to you. And..."

The birds stopped talking—their attention was diverted by a slight movement on the floor.

"Is that what I think it is?" asked Crystal.

A small twig seemed to be moving slowly toward the doves. "My condolences about your family tree. If there's anything I can do...."

"Xavier's back!" exclaimed Indy, obviously getting a kick out the chameleon's ability to blend with his surroundings. "I wish he could teach me that trick."

"Indy, you already know," he replied.

"What else can you share with us?" asked Crystal.

Xavier was delighted to see a more receptive audience. "Let me share the principle that has guided chameleons for generations—if you are open to it."

Without prompting, the birds gathered themselves in a semicircle around Xavier.

"You now recognize the four behavioral styles represented by each of your species," he began. "You're on the path to letting go of unrealistic expectations of one another. It also appears you've discovered that we all shine when we play to our strengths. Your next step is to pay attention to how you *treat* each other. I hold myself accountable to treat others how *they* need to be treated, not how *I* need to be treated."

Treat others how they *need to be treated,*
not how I *need to be treated.*

The birds studied him quizzically.

"I'm a bit confused," volunteered Crystal. "Doesn't this violate the 'Golden Rule': Treat others how *you* want to be treated?"

"Your point is well taken," said Xavier. "In terms of respect, honesty, and integrity, the Golden Rule holds true. But when working with others or simply communicating with them, should you treat them according to *your* needs or *theirs*? Think about it."

The chameleon flashed a grin and then slithered down the Council Tree. Within moments, he was gone.

Unsure what to do next, the Council sat in silence.

Then, Indy piped up. "There's big wisdom in that little lizard."

Everyone laughed—until Dorian brought them back to business. "Okay, that was interesting, but I'd like to shift our focus to the matter at hand—the trees."

"If I may," Clark interjected, "I believe that we are observing the four styles playing out right before our eyes. Before we continue, I'd like to understand the process that the parrots used to elicit information during their interviews. In addition, I'd like to share how I obtained data through observation. Rather than *start* with the bottom line of what we all found, I request that we describe our processes first, then *conclude* with the results. Would that be acceptable?"

Dorian took a deep breath, contemplating what Xavier had just taught them. "Okay, I guess I need to treat you the way you want to be treated. So, tough as it is for me to listen to the *whole process,* I will because it's important to you." He paused for a second and then added, "Truth be told, I guess it's important for me, too. I mean, I should learn about the process."

Sarah looked at Dorian with compassion. "I know what you mean. Samuel and I just experienced how exhausting it is to work out of our natural style. But I must say, being direct and projecting authority came in very handy last night. I guess we were tapping into the eagle style, as Xavier called it. Maybe our inner owl will help us, too."

"Know what?" Indy chirped. "Xavier's really onto something here! I mean, we could all benefit from treating others the way they want to be treated, right? Let's see…we already have the Golden Rule…why don't we call this the 'Home Rule?'"

"I like that," declared Sarah. "After all, when we treat others how *they* want to be treated, we make them feel right at home."

The Council was in agreement.

"So it is," declared Dorian, glancing at Clark to capture the Home Rule in the meeting minutes.

Already got it," he confirmed, without looking up.

"Parrots, you're up first," said Dorian. "Tell us what you discovered."

The parrots simultaneously fluttered over to the center limb of the Council Tree. Indy began excitedly, "It's all in the approach. So when I spoke to Donna the mountain lion, I just cut to the chase. I skipped all the small talk and got right down to business because her style is just like you, Dorian."

Dorian smirked, "Nobody is *just* like me!"

Ivy added, "The most important thing with Donna is to be direct and confident. Otherwise, she'll have you for lunch."

"Yeah, 'parrot cake with scream cheese frosting,'" Indy quipped.

Ivy and Indy laughed at their own joke.

"Okay, so what was the bottom line?" asked Dorian. "What did she tell you?"

"Not much," said Ivy.

"But at least we know that she doesn't know anything," said Indy.

"And she agreed to keep her ear to the ground and let us know if she hears anything," said Ivy.

"You persuaded a *mountain lion* to do that for you? That's impressive!" Dorian exclaimed. "For what it's worth, treat me like a mountain lion, and we'll be fine."

"I thought nobody is just like you," Indy taunted.

"Keep it up. You're beginning to look mighty tasty," Dorian deadpanned.

Indy continued, "Next, we ran into the deer, Sally and Sol, and their fawns. Such a nice family! Anyway, their style is like Samuel and Sarah's, so we were patient, soft-spoken, and sincere."

"Yeah," Ivy chimed in, "we didn't jump right into business. We enjoyed their company first and even played games with their little guys."

"Hold on," said Clark. "I don't mean to cast doubt on your methodology, but how could you gather information while playing games?"

"While we were playing games with the deer," replied Indy, "we were building an emotional connection so they would trust us with information."

"That sounds a bit like manipulation," expressed Crystal.

"Not at all," replied Ivy. "We were simply following the Home Rule without even realizing it! We just treated them how *they* like to be treated. And those kids play a mean game of hide-and-seek!"

"I'll tell you something," added Indy. "At first, the deer were very reluctant to talk about the crisis. We wanted them to feel comfortable. Otherwise, we wouldn't have learned anything."

"And...?" Dorian pressed.

"Man has not been sighted for over two weeks," Indy said casually.

"Now we're getting somewhere!" proclaimed Dorian. "Who was next?"

"Well, then we darn near flew into a swarm of worker bees. We didn't know any of them personally, so we had to be extra careful," said Ivy. "Bees are regimented and exacting...so, just like our owl friends, we spoke to them in a C style. We stayed factual and organized and made sure to provide them with sufficient background information."

"Whew," said Indy, wiping his brow. "*That* was exhausting."

"Makes sense to me," confirmed Clark. "But how did you know how to do all this? I mean, how did you know they were C's?"

"It was easy!" said Ivy. "They were all flying in perfect formation, spoke in a measured tone of voice, and shared only relevant facts and details. They were just like you Clark. And just like you Crystal. So we talked to them like we would talk to you. It worked! Applying the Home Rule is really easy if you just pay attention to what others do. Take us parrots. We're animated and upbeat most of the time. So if you want to connect with us, just schmooze and share a few laughs."

> *Applying the Home Rule is really easy if you*
> *just pay attention to what others do.*

"So that's how you do it," said Clark. "Indy, you were just like a chameleon. You made quick behavioral observations and then adapted your style to match the individual or the situation. You already knew the trick, just like Xavier said."

"That's so cool," replied Indy.

As the birds carried on, a brisk wind brought on a sudden chill. The birds instinctively moved from the end of the branch to the center of the tree for protection. Dorian noticed dark clouds gathering overhead.

"Anyway, it took a while," continued Indy, "but ultimately, our new bee friend, Cole, said that their hive was in the first tree that went down. It survived the crash but came apart when their branch got dragged through the creek and out to the Great Lake."

"What?!" Clark exclaimed. "The branches were removed from Tree #1?"

Indy nodded.

The owl, now visibly troubled, began pacing back and forth and then suddenly declared, "We have to go!"

"Where to?" asked Dorian.

"No time to explain," Clark shot back.

"But there's a storm coming," said Ivy.

Clark leapt from the branch and headed toward the open sky, followed immediately by Dorian. The parrots, doves, and Crystal stood wide-eyed, not sure what was happening. After a few seconds, Dorian looked back over his shoulder and commanded, "Let's go! Follow Clark."

As soon as they climbed above the trees, cold rain pelted the birds in a downpour. In mid-flight, Dorian turned to Clark and asked, "What's going on?"

"In preparation for our crash site analysis," shouted Clark, "we organized a comprehensive list of questions in order to reconstruct and compare what happened to each of the fallen trees, not just the most recent one."

A look of concern flashed across Dorian's face.

"Don't worry, my bottom-line friend," Clark chuckled. "We didn't spend *all* day doing this."

A crack of lightning suddenly flashed across the sky—a dangerous reminder of why birds shouldn't fly during a storm. The parrots struggled to navigate through wind gusts as the rain came down in sheets. The doves, who were the smallest of the group, barely kept up with the rest.

"C'mon, guys—we can make it through!" Ivy encouraged. "We can do this!"

A deafening thunderclap reverberated in every direction.

Clark resumed, shouting even louder over the storm, "We identified key areas of inquiry such as, 'Were the cut patterns on each tree the same?' 'Are we looking for more than one culprit?' 'Why were these particular trees under attack?' Crystal and I thought maybe their location had something to do with it."

"Clark, I am impressed," responded Dorian. "I truly am. But I'm also freezing my feathers off out here and would very much appreciate that bottom line!"

Clark obliged. "Almost immediately, we observed that branches were removed at Crash Site 2, but not from Samuel and Sarah's tree at Crash Site 3. Based on the parrots' evidence of the same pattern from Crash Site 1, I predict that the perpetrator will soon return to the doves' former tree to remove the branches and finish the job."

"And when they do," hollered Indy from behind, "we'll be there to catch 'em in the act!"

"Excellent work, Clark," said Dorian.

Sarah smiled. Maybe we can work as a team after all.

CHAPTER 12

The Stakeout

D renched and shivering, the birds tried their best to conceal their presence at Crash Site 3. Dorian, the largest member of the group, crouched uncomfortably behind the biggest trunk he could find.

"I have to say, Clark," said Dorian, "your meticulous nature has served us well. All those questions identified details and patterns I would have missed."

"Me, too," said Indy. "You know, I always thought you asked so many questions because you didn't trust us. Seems that you've just been trying to get the most accurate information."

"Well, of course!" responded Crystal. "We don't mean to offend anyone. It's just about getting it right. Exactly right, every time."

"*Exactly* right, *every* time?" laughed Dorian. "Life doesn't work that way for me. I'll take 'good enough' and move on to the next challenge."

Dorian shifted again, trying to get comfortable. Samuel watched him. The events of the past few days had brought out a bolder side of the dove, and there was something he wanted to say to the eagle.

"I've often interpreted your...abruptness as being disinterested in our opinions and feelings," conceded Samuel. "But after experiencing some eagle energy last night, I realize now that you simply want to solve problems as they arise so you can move on to the next one. It's not that you don't care—it's just that you're resolving the situation, not getting caught up in emotions."

"That's my nature," acknowledged Dorian. "And if you were able to utilize 'eagle energy,' as you called it, I guess I can learn to access some dove or owl energy when I need it."

Ivy laughed. "I tell ya', I bet we'll be flexing to each other's styles all the time now!"

"I don't know about *all the time*," said Crystal. "But it's clear that by simply observing others, we can identify their style and understand what makes them tick. And by understanding their intentions, we're less likely to judge them."

"Well said," agreed Clark, noting Crystal's observation.

It's clear that by simply observing others, we can identify their style and understand what makes them tick. And by understanding their intentions, we're less likely to judge them.

The birds remained at Crash Site 3 throughout the night, with the owls taking the evening shift. A light rain continued to fall, but the owls remained vigilant.

In the morning, the sky cleared and the air was illuminated by shafts of misty sunlight. Other forest residents began emerging from their protective cover. The owls jealously watched a few robins unearth some worms. Dorian spied a pack of wolves giving chase to a rabbit. Indy and Ivy were mesmerized by two squirrels spiraling up and down an adjacent tree.

"Make it a squirrel race!" shouted Indy.

"Shhhhhhh!" whispered Clark. "You're going to give away our location."

The birds quietly watched the sunrise as the morning chill gave way to a humid afternoon, and still, nothing materialized. The parrots could barely control their bottled-up energy, but they were the picture of tranquility compared to Dorian, who was stewing with resentment toward the unidentified perpetrator.

As the sky filled with reds and yellows, Dorian grew more and more impatient. "This is intolerable," he thought.

Then suddenly, it appeared.

Indy was the first to see it and elbowed Clark. "Hey, what's that?" he asked.

"I don't believe it," said Ivy.

"Of course!" said Clark. "Now it all makes sense! The branches. The wood chips. The proximity to the creek. It's a..."

"I'll be darned," interrupted Ivy.

"It's a beaver!" gasped Indy, loud enough to give away their location.

"We've never had beavers in our forest before," added Ivy. "Well, at least that explains why the wolves were there."

Everyone shot Indy a puzzled look.

"What?" he proclaimed. "They say beavers taste like chicken."

The beaver looked up and then continued gnawing branches off of what had been the dove family tree.

Dorian's eyes narrowed. "I'll take care of this!"

Samuel and Sarah simultaneously yelled, "Wait!"

Clark shouted, "Stop! Let's talk about this first before…. *uh-oh.*"

Dorian shot out from behind the tree as the rest of the birds watched helplessly. After a few moments, their fear turned into curiosity as they observed the spectacle unfolding from a safe distance.

Dorian was bearing down on the beaver, speaking forcefully.

"Look at that!" said Clark. "Nobody communicates with authority like Dorian. He's surely getting his message across."

The beaver dropped the branch he was munching on but did not respond to Dorian's piercing words and gaze. In response, the eagle grew even angrier, widely gesticulating and pointing at the downed tree.

"This does not look good," Indy cringed.

Dorian, now overcome with rage, threatened the beaver, who had picked up the branch again and resumed chewing.

"Whoa," asked Samuel, after seeing one of the eagle's talons joust near the the beaver "did Dorian just hit him?"

"Nah. He's just pointing at the downed tree," said Indy. "But on a persuasion scale of one to ten, with one meaning more trees will fall and ten being he convinced the beaver to stop cutting down our trees," I'd give Dorian..."

"A zero," remarked Ivy.

Dorian stood wide-eyed as the beaver tossed an indifferent glance over his shoulder before calmly swimming away.

"Why is Dorian continuing to shout while our prime suspect gets away?" asked Clark.

"Zero impact," Indy announced.

Landing in a furious swoop next to his friends, Dorian unleashed. "He ignored me!"

The eagle stomped around for a while and then yelled, "I gave that tree chopper a piece of my mind and he just swam away. Did you see that? He just swam away!"

"Dorian," said Clark, "chopping down trees is what beavers do."

"What, are you on *his* team now?" Dorian fumed. "That's exactly what *he* said. 'I'm a beaver. We cut down trees. That's what beavers do.' Well, I'll find him and take care of this."

"Whoa!" Indy's wing shot out, grabbing Dorian's shoulder. "Hold on a minute there, Big D. We need to regroup."

"We need a plan," said Clark.

"Let's all take a deep breath," said Sarah.

Dorian began to calm down and think this through. "Fine. I guess I didn't handle that as well as I could have," he conceded. "But what do you expect? I'm an eagle. I see something that needs to be done, and I do it. I don't spot a rabbit and *think* about it. I dive. I attack. I eat. That's what *eagles* do."

"Indeed," said a voice from under a nearby rock. "You were very assertive, but the question is: Was it the right style at the right time?"

Everyone turned to see what appeared to be a sliver of grey limestone gliding toward them.

"Xavier!" exclaimed Ivy. "Boy, am I glad to see you!"

Xavier smiled. "I heard about your stakeout and thought I'd see how things were going."

"Swell," Dorian snorted. "A beaver who thinks he's boss! Imagine! Now we know who's ripping our forest apart."

"Yes," the chameleon replied, "but how are you going to resolve the situation? After all, the beaver was just doing what—"

"I know, I know," Dorian muttered, "doing what beavers do."

Xavier looked sharply at the eagle, his voice firm. "Dorian, you have great strengths, but overusing your strengths won't deliver the results you seek."

The eagle raised an eyebrow.

"You're a *D* style," Xavier explained. "You communicate forcefully, achieving great clarity and purpose. Recall when the first tree crashed, you rallied the other birds and warned that another tree could fall soon. And you were right. Your directness spurred everyone into action."

Dorian nodded, his breathing slowing to its normal pace.

"That being said," the chameleon frowned, "you sometimes overuse your strengths. And when you do, those strengths become weaknesses."

You sometimes overuse your strengths. And when you do, those strengths become weaknesses.

Dorian appeared confused.

Xavier continued, "For example, your assertiveness becomes aggressiveness. Healthy confidence becomes arrogance. Taking the initiative morphs into steamrolling others before the best solution has even been identified. Ultimately, this weakens your ability to achieve your goals."

Dorian considered this for a moment and grudgingly nodded in agreement.

Xavier smiled. "But rest assured, my eagle friend, you're not alone."

Then, the he walked over to the owls.

Crystal grimaced. "Looks like we're next."

"As C's, your zest for asking questions, organizing details, and analyzing patterns allows you to structure your world, as in the case of your tree grid. However, when overused, the C style can lead to 'analysis paralysis,' like when you spent an entire day creating a massive list of interview questions."

Embarrassed, Clark and Crystal bowed their heads slightly.

"However, more recently, your crash site analysis brought out the best in you. Applied appropriately, your skills led to the culprit."

"Funny how others can see our faults so clearly!" said Indy. "Okay Xavier, now that you're all warmed up, the parrots have braced for impact. Go for it!"

Xavier obliged. "Indy, the I's gift for eternal optimism creates a lively atmosphere and fosters creativity. However, your natural cheerfulness can blind you to situations that are, in fact, quite dangerous. You were the first to discover Crash Site 1, yet you failed to recognize its significance or even report it."

"True," Ivy responded. "I guess that's because we don't see threats, we see opportunities."

"And it's that optimism that was reassuring as more trees started to come down. You believed that everything would be okay, and your encouragement helped to prevent widespread panic. That was helpful—very helpful."

Turning to the doves, Xavier began to speak, but was uncharacteristically interrupted by Sarah. "Let me guess," she smiled. "Our discomfort with conflict gets in the way of being honest and sharing our thoughts and ideas."

"Exactly!" interrupted Dorian. "During our Council meetings, I kept feeling like you had something to add, though you and Samuel didn't say much. But when you brought Xavier to help us out, it changed the way we interact. That was daring, and it worked."

Ivy chimed in. "I guess in 'overuse mode,' your S style was too passive. But when you acted on your need for harmony, it helped us all."

Xavier was proud of his students. "You don't need to change your style in order to be more effective," he added. "You just need to be able to tap into other styles when appropriate and to be careful about overusing your strengths."

You don't need to change your style in order to be more effective. You just need to be able to tap into other styles when appropriate and to be careful about overusing your strengths.

A soft breeze rustled the leaves of a nearby tree. The group stood for a moment in silence, feeling the warmth of the morning sun. Dawn had ended, and a new day had begun.

"So, what are you going to do now?" asked the chameleon.

Xavier flashed one of his famous grins, returned to a grey limestone color, and slithered away.

CHAPTER 13

The Gathering

One week later, the Council Tree hosted the largest assembly meeting in the forest's history. In attendance were more than three hundred birds representing Home's avian populations. The air was buzzing with speculation about what would happen next. One especially controversial rumor had the entire bird population moving to another forest to escape the specter of falling trees. Absolutely everyone was flapping about it.

Dorian stood up and spread his wings wide. The crowd grew silent. "As you all know, recent events have brought much concern to the inhabitants of Home. Therefore, I am extremely pleased to announce that we have reached an accord with the beavers. Your trees and nests are safe once again."

The audience erupted in wild applause as loose feathers filled the air, blanketing everything in a festive array of colors.

"I would like to recognize key contributions that have led to this historic resolution," continued Dorian. "Please join me in welcoming our heroic dove representatives, Samuel and Sarah, to the podium."

As the crowd cheered, the two doves reluctantly joined their eagle friend.

"These two don't like to be in the spotlight, but we're going to celebrate them anyway! It was Samuel and Sarah who reached out to the beavers and won their trust. They identified the beavers' fear of the wolves, and got the beavers to agree to stop chopping down the trees we live in if we could get the wolves off their backs."

The birds hooted and hollered, then Indy shouted out, "Dorian, tell 'em what you did next!"

"Well," Dorian chuckled, smirking mischievously, "let's just say that I spoke to the wolves as *they* like to be spoken to…and they won't be bothering the beavers anymore."

The audience roared with delight.

"There's more," the eagle continued as he waved his owl friends to the podium. "In order to coordinate with the beavers about which trees are safe to chop down and which ones to preserve, we needed an ingenious, foolproof plan. Nobody was better suited to design such a strategy than Clark and Crystal. They created a system to identify trees that are not inhabited by our population. If you plan on moving to a new tree, simply check with Clark and Crystal to verify that it's safe.

"Most impressively, we will now be identifying dying trees that aren't well suited for us anyway. Having the beavers chop them down actually strengthens the healthy trees that we like to nest in.

"The owls really thought this through, and let me tell you—I'm glad they're on the Home team!"

The owl audience members hooted happily as Clark and Crystal smiled at each other.

"And last, but definitely not least, I want to share something about Indy and Ivy," said Dorian. "Our parrot friends will play a major role in executing our agreement with the beavers. They will travel from nest to nest updating us about which trees are marked for beaver takedown. And, along with the doves, the parrots will continue to communicate with the beavers should any issues arise."

"And?" yelled Indy from high branch.

Dorian paused. He smiled and chuckled to himself. "And, these parrots have a motto that says, *"Life's no fun when there's work to be done. But we can make it better if we do it together."*

"And?" yelled Ivy.

Dorian paused again, still smiling. He cleared his throat. "I would like to propose that this becomes the official Home motto."

The crowd cheered loudly as two parrots simultaneously leapt from the upper branches and performed a perfectly synchronized Swan Dive, landing right next to Dorian. The entire audience began chanting the motto.

"Okay, okay—" Dorian began, attempting to keep the noise to a minimum. But he quickly realized there was no stopping the parrots or the crowd, so he shrugged and joined in.

Dorian gazed at the sea of fellow birds and a smile spread across his face. "Home is the best forest in all the land!" he proclaimed.

It was clear from the eruption of cheers that everyone agreed.

EPILOGUE

The Power of DISC

A week later, our heroes gathered at the Council Tree.

With a thoughtful look, Clark asked the group, "Xavier told us that the wisdom of the four styles was once known to all. How could something so powerful get lost over time? I would have assumed that the elder generations of owls would have created a system to preserve the…"

"It wasn't lost," said the parrot. "It's been right here in front of us all along. It's in our names!"

"I've always thought that each of our species selected names based on a specific letter because of tradition," said Sarah. "Now it's clear that the styles have been embedded in our culture, and we didn't even know it."

So the letters D, I, S, and C have more meaning than we thought," added Samuel.

The group all gazed into the distance as the sun crossed the horizon.

"I wonder if the styles hold true outside of Home," mused Crystal.

"Outside?" asked Indy.

"I'm thinking about one species in particular," said Crystal.

Clark nodded. "Man. Their names don't fit into any known system or pattern."

"But wouldn't it be easier for Man to figure out each other's styles if they used a code like ours?" asked Ivy.

Sarah answered, "They're a lot more complex than we are. Some act like eagles and others like parrots. Some behave like owls and others are like doves."

"Yeah," said Indy, "but here's the crazy part. I've watched them from above, and I can tell you, many are a combination of two of us—like parreagles or dovowls!"

"How confusing," said Dorian. "How do they get anything done?"

"Beats me," said Indy. "We may be complicated, but we're not *that* complicated!"

"This is important," Dorian added. "We should take steps to ensure this knowledge gets passed down to future generations."

They all agreed and worked together to recap what they had learned as Clark wrote down the ideas on a parchment scroll. Clark spoke as he began writing. "Let's call this the Preservation of Wisdom of the Four Styles Act so that all current and future..."

"Clark?" Dorian interrupted. "How about we just call it *DISC*?"

Clark grinned and nodded. "Brevity. I can live with that."

"Now, if there is no further business, I, for one, am looking forward to the doves' Tree-Warming Party," said Crystal.

"I can't wait," said Ivy. "We've got a few surprises for you."

"Does this mean we're going to find out what happens at your famous Happy Hours?" asked Sarah.

"You got it!" smiled Indy. "But as Xavier once advised, 'Be careful what you ask for....'"

Taking flight, they laughed and rose into the sunset.

PART II

The *DISC* Model

There are four important points to consider as we delve into the world of the *DISC* styles.

First, all styles are positive and contribute to the world in meaningful ways. In the fable, Dorian's *D* style directness was as essential to the bird's success as Sarah's *S* style sensitivity. Indy's *I* style communication skills were no more or less important than Clark's *C* style drive for accuracy and precision. Each style possesses unique strengths and capabilities that should be celebrated. Simply put, there is no "best" style.

Second, there's no need to change the core essence of who you are. That would be exchanging one set of potential strengths and challenges for another. Imagine Dorian trying to completely morph into an *S* style dove or Crystal seeking to become an *I* style parrot. Embracing the styles means fully recognizing and accepting your natural gifts.

Third, nobody is just one style. We are each a combination of all four. Unlike our bird friends who neatly fit into one style, people are far more complex, and this makes each of us unique.

And fourth, we each have the capacity to adapt to different situations through style flexibility. By tapping into the abilities of all four styles, we build healthier and happier relationships and achieve our highest potential.

GO ONLINE TO DISCOVER YOUR STYLE

Before you read on, we urge you to take a few minutes to go to www.TakeFlightLearning.com and complete a *free* mini *DISC* assessment. Through this 15 question survey, you will receive a brief description of your natural strengths and challenges based upon your *DISC* style.

You also have the option to receive a comprehensive *Taking Flight! DISC* report. To obtain this in-depth analysis, enter the code, *teachmemore,* for a special discounted rate. You will be joining millions of people worldwide who have accessed this report to unlock their personal potential and learn to communicate with any style in the workplace, home, or school environment.

This revealing report includes:

- A graph that shows your primary and secondary *DISC* styles.

- A detailed description of your style and your strengths.

- How you are likely to communicate with others and the dos and don'ts of communicating with you.

- Your greatest "fears" in relationships so you can avoid having others "push your buttons."

- Your compatibility with people of other styles. You will begin to understand why you are instinctively drawn to certain styles and why you avoid others.

- Great historical figures that match your profile. There is no wrong or right style—great leaders come from every style.

- Your strengths as a leader and how to use this to achieve success.

- A personalized action plan for applying *DISC* in your life.

Remember, there is no "best" style. Each style has its strengths and challenges. Further, style is not a predictor of success or happiness. People of every *DISC* style combination have healthy relationships and live fulfilling lives.

THE HISTORY AND MYSTERY OF THE
FOUR STYLES

Now that you better understand your behavioral style, let's place it in some context. The wisdom of styles has existed for millennia. Twenty-four hundred years ago, Hippocrates described four humours, and Aristotle, four elements. Variations of the four styles continued to appear over the centuries. In modern times, Carl Jung identified four functions; Eduard Spränger, four value attitudes; Erich Fromm, four orientations. Even Pavlov noted four temperaments—and he was studying dogs! In his 1928 book, *The Emotions of Normal People*, William Marston designated four styles beginning with the letters *D*, *I*, *S*, and *C*. Marston freely offered the *DISC* styles to the world allowing them to be used without the burden of copyright restrictions. Today, millions of people across the globe have taken *DISC* profiles.

So, how is it that the styles have remained consistent for thousands of years, across continents and cultures, in people and in animals? The answer was finally revealed when researchers observed that the four quadrants of the brain generally correspond to specific behavioral patterns. Our brains' hardwiring drives how we think, feel, and act, which in turn defines who we are.

Four brain quadrants—four styles. It's that simple.

THE FOUR STYLES

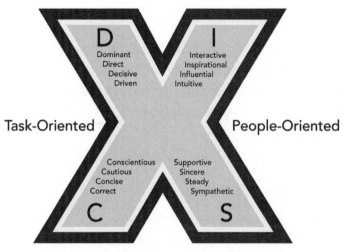

Fast-Paced, Verbal

D
Dominant
Direct
Decisive
Driven

I
Interactive
Inspirational
Influential
Intuitive

Task-Oriented

People-Oriented

Conscientious
Cautious
Concise
Correct

Supportive
Sincere
Steady
Sympathetic

C

S

Even-Paced, Reserved

The Dominant *D* Style

Like Dorian the eagle, *D's* focus on achieving results. They favor action over planning and are typically guided by a long-term, big-picture vision of what can be accomplished. *D's* seek challenges and take risks that will yield big rewards. They can quickly size up a situation and decisively determine a course of action.

D's are assertive, direct, and competitive. They don't like to waste time, and their bottom-line nature drives how they communicate. They want straight answers and "call it like it is."

D's are self-starters who challenge the status quo. They thrive in positions of power and seek to control their own destinies. Their tenacity and natural confidence enable them to accomplish even the most demanding objectives.

The Interactive *I* Style

Like the parrots, Indy and Ivy, *I's* have active minds, seek constant stimulation, and enjoy interacting with people and the world around them. This allows them to thrive in social environments and drives their thirst for adventure.

With their boundless optimism and innate people skills, *I's* are highly persuasive and inspirational. They have fun wherever they go and infuse play and positive energy into all aspects of their lives.

The *I's* intuition and free-spirited nature enable them to create "out of the box" ideas. They don't get bogged down in minutiae, as details would only restrict their imagination. *I's* are future-focused and live in the realm of possibility, where everything is exciting and achievable.

The Supportive **S** Style

Just as doves Samuel and Sarah sought to restore harmony to Home, *S's* seek to minimize conflict and create calm, safe environments. *S's* are friendly, compassionate people who patiently listen with empathy. They build deep, loyal relationships and are steadfast friends and partners.

S's favor practical, tried-and-true procedures that ensure stability. They like familiar, predictable patterns that produce consistent and reliable outcomes. They often work behind the scenes and prefer to support, rather than to lead.

The Conscientious **C** Style

 As with owls Clark and Crystal, *C's* focus on achieving complete accuracy in everything they do. They constantly question processes and ideas to ensure that things are done properly. *C's* are systematic, detail-oriented, and efficient.

Rather than being guided by the emotion of a situation, *C's* make practical decisions based on logical analysis of observable, quantifiable information. Although *C's* often prefer to work independently, their even-tempered nature enables them to remain objective and diplomatic when dealing with others.

STYLE COMBINATIONS AVAILABLE
IN THE APPENDIX

It's important to recognize that each of us has a blend of all the styles. In addition to our strongest or primary style, many people also have a prominent secondary style. Check out the Appendix to learn how the *DISC* styles combine to paint a more holistic picture of your overall personality.

PEOPLE READING

You enter a local restaurant and immediately notice your waitress's beaming grin and easy laugh. You watch how effortlessly she strikes up a conversation about last night's football game. She actually seems excited about what you've ordered and enthusiastically places it before you. She quickly greets another customer passing by, and all the while, she never stops smiling. You've likely identified your waitress as an *I*.

Wouldn't it be great if you could figure out someone's *DISC* style within a few minutes of meeting the person? Imagine how much easier it would be to communicate with your manager if you knew she was a *D*. How much more could you sell if you recognized your customer as an *I*? How would it impact your career if you realized that the person interviewing you was a *C*? And how much more effective would you be as a leader if you determined that you were managing a group of *S*'s?

When observing others from a *DISC* perspective, each piece of the puzzle spontaneously assembles into an easily definable picture—a quick roadmap of how you should interact with them. You can simply observe how others behave, how they move, the way they speak, and it all comes together.

Tune into people's words, tone, and body language. Are they animated or subdued? Rigid or relaxed? Is their tone upbeat and dynamic or soft and flat? Do they speak quickly and spontaneously or slowly and measured? Do they make definitive statements that convey confidence, or do they ask questions to assure understanding? Pay attention to how they listen. Do they validate emotions with empathy, or are they impatient listeners who interrupt with their own ideas?

All of these characteristics are aspects of the behavioral style puzzle. The more you practice tuning into the pieces, the more adept you will become at identifying *DISC* styles. Most people find that after a few weeks of observing the styles of friends, family, or even characters on television shows or in movies, they can identify the styles of people they have just met—in minutes, or even less.

Consider the following observable signs of people with each of the four styles:

Dominant—The first sign that someone is a D is that he or she exudes self-confidence of an eagle. *D's* stand tall, have firm handshakes, and maintain steady eye contact. *D's* tones of voice are assertive and direct. They speak with such certainty that even when sharing new ideas, *D's* can come across as experts. *D's* jump right to the matter at hand and dispense with the niceties. They call it like it is. Not to be bothered with fluff, they cut to the chase and ask for what they want. If you are providing too much detail, you might notice a *D's* impatience as he directs the conversation to the bottom line. You may also find that, at best, *D's* provide suggestions about how you should handle situations or solve problems. At worst, they impose their opinions or even their will upon you.

Interactive—The big smile, wide eyes, and hearty laugh that can fill a room are dead giveaways that you've encountered the parrot energy of an *I*. In fact, you might find *I*'s laugh at their own jokes even more than their audience! They often use their full bodies to emphasize their excitement or to make a point, casually taking up lots of physical space. When *I*'s speak, their tones range from happy to excited. Even small experiences are larger-than-life events for *I*'s. If something is good, to an *I* it's great! If it's bad, it's horrible. Look for *I*'s to comfortably start conversations with strangers, as they are energized by unfamiliar or large groups. They can build rapport easily, and within minutes they'll be talking to you as if they've known you for years. *I*'s seem to have stories for every topic. At times it can even seem as if they need to "one up" whatever you have to say, but it's just the *I*'s way of connecting with you.

Supportive—When you meet an *S*, you'll immediately notice that he or she radiates a dove's sense of calm. The *S*'s soft smile and gentle touch reveals a mild, sincere demeanor. Their tone is friendly and nurturing, and their volume is quiet as they rarely raise their voices, even when angry. They move deliberately and use a small range of gestures, careful not to take up too much physical space. *S*'s shine in one-on-one interactions or in small, familiar groups. In these comfortable settings, they may be quite verbal and involved. However, in new or large groups, *S*'s can easily be overlooked given their quiet, unobtrusive manner. When they sense that others are not well, you can see how effortlessly they tune into emotions and lend an empathetic ear.

Conscientious—You can immediately identify a strong C through their owl-like nondemonstrative, restrained movements. Their facial expressions will often be flat, unemotional, and consistent. *C's* are sensitive to physical space. They're not likely to pat your back or offer a hug. They speak with their arms at their sides, rarely using them expressively as an *I* would. *C's* will typically make strong eye contact but will rarely nod their heads, smile, or give off cues that they agree or disagree with you, making them difficult to read. However, *C's* are patient listeners and will let you finish before they talk. And when they do, notice the level of detail they share, as well as the reasoning behind a decision or recommendation. *C's* favor logic over feelings and will relate even personal stories through facts and data. *C's* speak with intention, thus their words are measured and precise. Not comfortable with ambiguity, *C's* will ask lots of questions to ensure complete understanding.

SEVEN TRANSFORMATIVE DISC PRINCIPLES

In matters of style, swim with the current.
In matters of principle, stand like a rock.
—Thomas Jefferson

This section features seven *DISC* principles that will deepen your understanding of how to best internalize and apply the styles. Taken collectively, these principles provide a complete framework for understanding how the *DISC* can positively impact your life.

Principle 1—Understand Your Own Style

According to Aristotle, "Knowing yourself is the beginning of all wisdom." Why is this so important? Numerous studies indicate that individuals who score high in self-awareness are happier and achieve greater success than those who lack it. Self-awareness enables people to build their lives around their strengths and better manage their challenges.

Example: Jennifer worked in a customer service department where she handled incoming calls. Her role involved patiently listening to customer issues, sympathizing with their perspective, and processing their complaints through a complex database. Before long, Jennifer felt as though she were repeating the same call over and over again. Although the job itself wasn't challenging, she found herself exhausted and stressed at the end of each day.

Following a *DISC* training program, Jennifer realized why she was so unhappy: She was a *D* working in an *S* job. Today, she is still at the company but now thrives as a sales representative where she sets and pursues competitive goals with passion and perseverance. In sales, Jennifer can take risks and use her direct and assertive nature to get results. Not only does she love her new position, but her company has benefited twice: first by filling Jennifer's former job with an *S* who enjoys empathetically helping people, and again by placing Jennifer in a style-appropriate role.

Have you ever known someone who consistently struggles with his or her career or has had many contentious relationships? Having worked with thousands of people from all walks of life, we see this scenario on a regular basis. The common denominator is often that these individuals are out of touch with their own behavioral styles. Consequently, they make critically important personal and professional decisions without considering how their brains are wired.

Have you ever been in a situation that you believe should be easy for you, but for some reason it is overwhelming or challenging? Maybe you accepted an interim job simply to pay the bills after a layoff. Perhaps you assumed a volunteer role because you believe in a cause, but the tasks involved were far more taxing than you imagined. Or maybe you took on new responsibilities at work that you believed would lead you to the next level but you found an aspect of the new job simply exhausting.

Knowing ourselves and paying close attention to situations where we either feel energized or exhausted can help us make decisions that enable our strengths to shine and minimize situations that rely too heavily upon our weaknesses.

Principle 2—Recognize the Styles of Others

Sun Tzu said, "If you know the enemy and know yourself, you need not fear a hundred battles."

So how do you identify others' styles? Just ask yourself these questions: Are they fast-paced or even-paced? Are they outgoing or reserved? Are they detail-oriented or big-picture? Are they risk-takers or cautious? Are they planned or spontaneous? Each answer fills in a piece of the style puzzle.

The more you practice answering these questions about people, the more intuitive you will become in recognizing the styles of others. In time, you'll be able to identify styles with ease. In fact, we'll bet that you've already developed people-reading skills. Let's give it a try. What styles best define the following people: Donald Trump, Robin Williams, Princess Diana, and Bill Gates? Think about it for just a moment before you read on.

If you said *D*, *I*, *S*, and *C*, respectively, you're well on your way to recognizing the styles.

In our daily lives, being skilled in "people-reading" enables you to better leverage other people's strengths.

For example, consider Maria. She is a reserved, soft-spoken S. She needed to purchase a new car but dreaded the idea of bargaining with a salesperson. While speaking with her sister, Jane, she realized that Jane's persuasive I style would be more adept at haggling for a great deal than her own S style. In the end, Jane got Maria a great price on the car and was even energized by the experience. Maria was relieved and grateful that she didn't have to negotiate the deal.

By recognizing the styles of others, you can leverage each others' strengths. In doing so, you utilize the power of the DISC styles to create true partnerships. Whether it's a coworker, spouse, child, or friend, understanding others is the foundation for strong relationships, better results, and a more fulfilling life.

Principle 3—Think About Style When Establishing Expectations

We all view the world through the lens of our own behavioral styles. Consequently, each one of us has expectations that are driven by our own style rather than by the styles of others. For example, we expect others to like what we like and need what we need. We assume people can do what we can do, and they will react as we would react. And we assume that the people in our lives understand our needs and will fulfill them ... *without our having to express them.* After all, shouldn't they already *know* what we want?

Example: Jasmine and Steve worked in adjacent cubicles at a major bank. The problem was that Steve played his music too loudly—or at least that's what Jasmine thought. A strong *D*, Steve assumed that if Jasmine didn't like his music, she'd pop her head over his cubicle and say so. But she never mentioned it. In reality, Jasmine, a strong *S*, had been stewing over his apparent lack of respect. "He *must* know it bothers me," she thought, "but he obviously doesn't care."

Weeks passed, and Jasmine grew increasingly annoyed. She complained to her husband, who suggested that she talk to Steve, but she was reluctant. "He should know better and just stop playing the music!" she protested. Another week passed, and finally Jasmine couldn't take it anymore and decided to give Steve a piece of her mind. "How do you concentrate with that music?" she asked, to which he replied, "I like it."

This only frustrated Jasmine even more.

Both Jasmine and Steve were trapped in their styles, unable to see the others' perspectives. Steve thought that if the music bothered Jasmine, she would just tell him. And why not? For a D, it's no big deal to address issues directly because they don't perceive direct communication as conflict, but as simply making a request. It's not an argument, it's a conversation.

As for Jasmine, her S-guided sensitivity couldn't relate to how Steve was behaving because she would never do such a thing. Yet she was not about to start a conflict with someone—especially over music. Besides, in her mind, she *did* address it with him, and she didn't want him to feel attacked.

Of course, Jasmine's indirect request lacked the assertiveness that would spur Steve to act. *D's* are direct about their needs and expect others to be direct as well. They don't perceive a direct statement as an attack. They actually appreciate the direct action or language. They expect it.

Unrealistic expectations lead to disappointment, poor results, ineffective decision making, increased conflict, and resentment. Fortunately, style awareness allows you to establish *realistic* expectations. By understanding your own style, recognizing the styles of others, and establishing expectations based upon what *others* need, both parties are likely to get their needs met.

Principle 4—Consider Intention, Not Just Behavior

We judge ourselves by our intentions and others by their actions. However, by better understanding the intentions of others, we can prevent misinterpretation and take the sting out of actions that could otherwise feel hurtful.

Example: One morning, Jake, a marketing executive, called George, his associate, into his office to delegate a critical project. Following their 90-minute meeting, Jake, true to his C style, felt confident that George had all of the information he needed to be successful. George, an I, felt quite differently. Jake had restricted him with so many processes and details that there was no room for George to think for himself or create something new. He left feeling frustrated and resentful.

"Why doesn't Jake just do it himself?" George thought. "After a year in this job, he still doesn't trust me or else he would have simply handed off the project and let me figure it out. What a micromanager." Soon after, George began looking for another job.

What happened in this situation? By not understanding his boss's style, George incorrectly assumed Jake's intent. In actuality, Jake trusted George completely. That's why he selected him to lead such an important project. His goal was simply to ensure that George had all of the tools he needed to be successful. Had Jake recognized George's style, he would have simply stated the goal, outlined the project, and let George move forward as he saw fit.

As for George, if he understood that Jake's intention was really just to be helpful, he wouldn't have felt micromanaged and mistrusted.

The *DISC* model is a powerful tool for understanding intentions and recognizing the source of behaviors that might otherwise irritate you. However, just because you understand someone's intent doesn't mean that you should tolerate disrespect, poor quality, or failure to achieve results. Positive intentions do not justify using style as a weapon. Jake shouldn't excuse his behavior by saying, "I'm a C and that means I provide a lot of information and structure. Deal with it."

People usually aim to satisfy *their own* needs, not to push *your* buttons. In other words, they do things *for* themselves, not *against* you. So the next time you experience a difficult conversation or engage in conflict, consider that you may be misreading the other person's intention.

Principle 5—Use Your Strengths but Don't Overuse Them

Too much of a good thing is *not* a good thing. When a strength is overused, it becomes a weakness. And while each of the DISC styles is inherently positive, when carried to an extreme, any style can become a disadvantage.

Example: Kate, a strong C, walked through her front door with six bags of groceries and a plan. It was 9:00 a.m., and 18 guests would be arriving later that afternoon for their annual holiday dinner.

Although Kate had several days to prepare for the event, she used a good deal of that time to organize the menu and identify tasks that needed to be accomplished to get the house in order. When she was finally ready to put her plan into action, she had a long list of to-dos and little time to implement them.

As soon as she reached the kitchen, Kate's husband, Mark—an intuitive I—immediately sensed her stress level and offered, "Relax, babe. It's just my parents and my sisters' families. What can we do to help?"

Kate was already feeling overwhelmed. In the past, she had delegated tasks to Mark, but they were rarely done according to her standards, and it usually meant that she had to do them herself anyway. She was reluctant to take him up on his offer to assist, but with so much to be done she asked him to set the dining room table. Off he went. A few minutes later Mark returned with a cheerful, "What's next?"

Skeptical that he could finish so quickly, Kate went in to inspect, sighed, and simply said, "Don't worry, I'll do it."

"But it's already done," Mark thought to himself as he raised his hands in confusion. Evidently, he had used the wrong tablecloth and napkins for this holiday, put the water glasses on the incorrect side, placed trivets in the wrong places, and didn't consider that two of the kids shouldn't receive the fine china.

"They won't care," comforted Mark. "It's my family. This looks fine."

"Just straighten up the living room and I'll fix the dining room."

By 1:30 p.m., Kate moved quickly from one task to the next, as she sensed the impending arrival of her guests. There was still much to be done: rosemary chicken, sweet potatoes, and asparagus in the oven, a pot of homemade tomato bisque on the stovetop, and a half-completed salad on the counter.

Mark, trying to stay out of the line of fire, approached the kitchen to check Kate's progress. "Hey, we're almost ready," he declared.

"Almost ready?" Kate shot back with a glare. "Do you know how much more we have to do? All of the food needs to be placed in the right dishes. The counters need to be wiped clean. The living room is still a mess!"

Nevertheless, by the time the guests arrived, all of the pieces were in place. Afterward, Mark's mother commented, "Everything was wonderful. What a lovely evening."

However, as Kate reflected on the night, her stomach tightened. She had forgotten to serve one of the desserts, the soup was a bit salty, and she failed to replace the tablecloth that Mark incorrectly put on the dining room table. "If only Mark would have been more helpful," she thought.

Kate's *C* enabled her to organize a beautiful dinner. However, the tight deadline caused by her excessive planning drove Kate to overuse her style, and she became stressed and inflexible. By seeking perfection, she elevated both her and her husband's stress level over an event that was supposed to be enjoyable. Instead of accepting help to reduce her stress, Kate alienated her partner by being overly critical. In the end, the meal was a success, but at a high emotional cost.

Although some people overuse their style on a regular basis, most of us overdo it during times of stress or uncertainty. Style excess can also be driven by emotionally charged situations or dysfunctional relationships. But no matter the cause, too much of any style creates added stress for everyone involved. Here's a brief overview of the darker side, or overuse, of style.

When *D*'s overuse their style, their interpersonal skills take a back seat to achieving results. Their directness turns blunt, abrasive, and insensitive. In the extreme, the *D*'s take-charge mind-set becomes overly demanding and domineering. Their confidence degenerates to stubborn, closed-minded arrogance as they steamroll over anyone who interferes with achieving their objectives.

When *I*'s overuse their style, their optimism can lead to unrealistic, impractical ideas, where gut feelings take precedence over reality and their enthusiasm comes across as superficial. Lacking essential facts and details, *I*'s can lean on exaggeration and manipulation to persuade others. Under stress, *I*'s often appear disorganized, manage their time poorly, and simply try to talk their way out of difficult situations instead of executing the plan.

When *S*'s overuse their style, their need for harmony leads to an avoidance of difficult conversations and healthy conflict. Their deep comfort with the status quo can also lead to complacency and a resistance to change. This causes them to become passive and dependent. When *S*'s don't get their needs met, they can become resentful and develop a victim mentality. In overuse mode, *S*'s simply wait for instruction from others and therefore appear fearful and unsure of themselves.

When *C's* overuse their style, their drive for quality and structure degenerates into perfectionism. They become so picky and critical that nothing meets their standards or gets accomplished. This makes them seem indecisive and rigid. Their need to question everything can lead to pessimism and resistance to new ideas. Their intense focus on the task can blind them to healthy delegation opportunities and place significant pressure on *C's* to do everything themselves.

Principle 6—Apply the Right Style at the Right Time

In the fable, Xavier understood that adaptability was the key to survival. Being a chameleon, he adjusted naturally to his surroundings and connected with everyone. In our own lives, we too can reap the benefits of accurately reading people and situations and then tapping into the right style at the right time. When we don't, we fail to meet objectives and are surprised by how others perceive us.

Example: It was a big day for Spencer, who was about to lead a sales presentation that could result in significant revenues for his firm. Joanne, the company president, greeted him with a quick handshake and said, "Tell me about your organization and what you can do for us."

Spencer opened with his professional background and a brief overview of his company. His primary objective was to establish rapport. After all, his strength was in building relationships.

It didn't take long for Spencer to discover that he had grown up just a town away from Joanne. They swapped childhood stories and reminisced about the good old days.

Next, Spencer unveiled a dazzling PowerPoint presentation that featured eye-popping graphics and a compelling vision. Joanne smiled throughout. Spencer closed by reassuring Joanne that his company had worked on many projects of this magnitude and that they would do a great job if selected. Driving back to the office, he felt he had made a strong impression.

One week later, Spencer was devastated to learn that a competitor had won the account. Joanne remarked to Spencer's boss that while he gave an energetic and appealing presentation, it didn't inspire her confidence that the job would get done. She wanted steak, and all he delivered was sizzle. Joanne had wanted to learn more about his company could do, not about Spencer.

Spencer's mistake: He treated Joanne like a fellow *I* when she was, in fact, a *D*. His failure to read her style correctly and adapt to it, created a losing situation from the start.

Most people have one style that they use too often and one that they don't use enough. Each style is needed at one time or another. The key is to be flexible enough to exhibit the right style at the right time.

Principle 7—Treat Others How They Need to Be Treated, Not How You Need to Be Treated (The "Home Rule")

We're all familiar with the Golden Rule—treat others the way you want to be treated. This universal principle can be traced back to a wide range of world cultures and religions. The Golden Rule is the foundation for meaningful relationships and cohesive societies when expressed through timeless values such as honesty, integrity, and respect.

However, as we learned in principle #5 about overuse, anything carried to an extreme can become a detriment. The Golden Rule is so ingrained in our thinking that we apply it universally... and that gets us into trouble. The "Home Rule" that we learned in the birds' story—treat others the way *they* need to be treated—is a much more effective strategy when it comes to communication and working together to achieve shared outcomes.

Example: Bashir, VP of Information Technology at a large insurance company, sought to roll out a major software upgrade throughout the organization. A year prior, however, his predecessor had experienced massive struggles with a very similar project, leading to cost overruns and disapproval from senior management. Working with the same staff, whose memory of the previous debacle was still fresh, Bashir needed this project to run smoothly.

To achieve a high level of buy-in, Bashir resisted a natural tendency to communicate solely within his S style. Instead, he intuitively recognized the need to connect with the full range of styles represented by his staff. One department at a time, Bashir gathered employees to explain the new system, fluidly adapting to each of the four styles like a chameleon.

When Bashir opened with, "Here's the executive summary," he immediately captured the *D's* attention by providing the bottom-line impact. For the *I's*, he turned on the enthusiasm: "You're going to love this system. It's cutting-edge...better than anything you've ever seen!" They left feeling excited and eager to use the new system. Bashir validated the *S's* perspective by revealing his own resistance to change: "I realize that this represents a big transition and that might be stressful, so we'll be offering support throughout the process to allay concerns as they arise." To address the *C's* priorities, who were feverishly taking notes on the PowerPoint handout, Bashir spoke in a measured tone and laid out a comprehensive, coherent plan. He encouraged them to ask questions and patiently answered each one. They emerged confident that the new system was well thought-out.

Bashir left each meeting feeling a bit drained, as he had worked outside of his style for much of the time. But it was worth it. He had created an army of change agents who had bought into the new system. After meeting with Bashir, the *D's* got the bottom line, the *I's* were energized, the *S's* were reassured, and the *C's* got the specifics they needed. The upgrade was implemented with great ease and minimal stress for everyone involved.

As Danish physicist Niels Bohr noted, "The opposite of a profound truth may well be another profound truth." So it is with the Golden Rule and the Home Rule. Both reinforce the notion that we should honor people for who they are and respect their needs and differences.

PART III

Taking Flight!
DISC for College Students

There is a saying that a person at college learns more outside the classroom than in it. That holds true whether you attend a university, a community college, or even a corporate learning program. By necessity, you will have to invest time, money, and effort toward the chance of an improved life as the result of any schooling. You may have to work a job, balance home life and school time, and even take care of children, a spouse, or other family members. Even for those able to concentrate fully on their studies, life has a way of crowding in when your car breaks down, you have relationship conflicts, or you face situations ranging from distractions to disasters.

Whether you come straight from high school or from a mid-life family or the military, you will have to acquire new skills in addition to gathering information in classes. You will need to manage money, manage time, and manage your own life and interactions with a varied assortment of other people with quite different styles. Knowing yourself and others through an awareness of the *DISC* styles can give you a real boost. Let us examine why in some real-life scenarios.

PAYING FOR SCHOOL

One of the greatest sources of conflict in relationships is finances. For married students who attend school later in life, balancing college tuition with life's daily expenses can be challenging—especially for partners who have different style perspectives. How far will either partner stretch his or her comfort zone to accommodate the other regarding financial security? Yet, money is often not at the heart of these issues. The real battle is rooted in fear and control.

If one partner seeks to live with certainty that bills will be paid and the other is willing to accept a higher level of ambiguity about how they will get by, conflict often arises. A powerful way to benefit from *DISC* awareness in relationships is to appreciate what each style both fears and seeks to control.

Example: Dawn and Jeff are sitting at the dinner table, going over the bills. Jeff is about to start school at a local college where he will be studying computer science. It was a difficult decision for Jeff to leave his job and go back to school, but the prospect of starting a family necessitated a more stable and lucrative career change.

As Dawn read through the tuition bills for first time, she found herself becoming anxious.

"I'm worried about where we're headed," she said. "We need to cut back."

"What do you mean?" asked Jeff. "We've been saving for this. We just need to follow the plan."

"What about the vacation last month?" asked Dawn. "We spent way more than we budgeted."

"That was an exception," replied Jeff. "It was the first vacation in a long time, and it was great."

"But what are we going to do now?" worried Dawn. "As of today we are $32,483 in debt, and that doesn't count our mortgage and car payments."

"If it gets bad, we can always take out a second mortgage. We've done that before. We'll be fine," reassured Jeff.

"That's exactly my point," replied Dawn. "We keep doing this to ourselves. Look at these vacation expenses. We really didn't need to stay in a 4-star hotel and we barely used the rental car, which cost us $375 plus the late fee."

"Forget about the late fee. How many times do we have to need to talk about that? We got a great deal on the rooms. And if you felt so strongly about this, why didn't you just change the hotels before the trip? You said nothing then and *now* you're freaking out?"

"Okay, fine. But look at this credit card bill. See how much you spend on lunch alone?" said Dawn.

"Come on. Now you're getting carried away. You want me to brown bag my lunch? Why don't we come up with a solution instead of obsessing about the problem?" replied Jeff.

"I did," responded Dawn "I just saved us $8 a day, which is $40 a week or $160 a month, which equals $1,920 a year!"

"That's an inconvenience. It doesn't solve the problem," said Jeff.

"It's a start, isn't it?" asked Dawn.

"The *solution* would be a way to bring in more income. Let's brainstorm that!" suggested Jeff.

"I'll make you a deal. Let's look for ways to supplement our income, and in exchange you bring your lunch for the next year…and I'll even make it for you half the time," said Dawn.

Jeff paused for moment. "Okay, and you're right. $1,920 a year *would* make a dent."

You probably guessed that Dawn is the analytical *C* style and Jeff is an optimistic *I*. Their style differences led to contrasting perspectives on how to solve the problem. Dawn's *C* energy sought to keep the couple financially safe. Jeff's *I* style wanted to cheer up Dawn by downplaying the severity of the situation. However, because they had different *DISC* styles and therefore, different approaches to how they handled money, they ended up in conflict.

C's fear chaos. The more inevitable the crisis, the more they will strive to construct systems to steer clear of the predicament. For Dawn, the money drain was an undisciplined situation that required controls. By paying attention to the details and analyzing patterns, *C*'s seek to create as much certainty and predictability as possible in their world.

I's do not fear chaos. For them, tough financial circumstances are an opportunity to make a change for the better or to try something new. The real issue, as perceived by Jeff, was a lack of imagination. Cutting back on expenses was merely addressing the symptom, not the problem. Jeff's abundance mentality sought to increase income, not contain expenses. What do *I*'s fear? Constraint. Jeff resisted being controlled, and his optimistic instincts fueled confidence that they would find a way to make it work.

Paying for school can bring much stress into a relationship. However, by understanding the *DISC* styles, couples can anticipate their partner's fears and address them from a place of understanding as opposed to judgment. In addition, both partners can leverage the perspective of the other to maximize what they both bring to the table.

DEALING WITH ROOMMATES

The transition from high school to college involves major life changes, such as moving out of the house, juggling a heavy workload, shopping for food, and doing your own laundry. But one of the biggest adjustments is often overlooked: Living in a dorm room with a complete stranger! After years of negotiating living relationships with siblings, college roommates have to learn to live with someone who may have the opposite idea of what represents "normal" behavior.

Example: As part of a student housing program to help new roommates start off on the right foot, dorm residents took *DISC* profiles and met with their Resident Assistant (RA) to go over the results.

By the time the RA got around to meeting with Logan and Noah, issues had already begun to surface. Following a quick recap of the previous night's basketball game, the RA turned the conversation to their *DISC* styles. "So, guys, did you have a chance to read your reports?"

"Yeah," replied Logan. "I'm definitely an *I* with some *D* thrown in there."

"And how about you, Noah," asked the RA.

"I'm a *C* with a secondary *S* style," replied Noah.

Based on the RA's suggestion, Logan and Noah then traded *DISC* reports so each could better understand his roommate. After several minutes, Logan announced, "I must be driving you crazy!"

"I have to say, there have been times when I didn't appreciate having ten people hanging out in our room," said Noah.

"But we included you," replied Logan.

"It's not about being included or excluded," said Noah. "I just wanted quiet."

"You came to college to be quiet?" asked Logan.

"Well, I'm usually quiet, so, yeah. And sometimes I need my space, and my own room seems like a reasonable place to have it," said Noah.

The RA turned to them both and asked, "Do you think your *DISC* styles have anything to do with this?"

"Everything!" said Logan. "We are so opposite."

"I think you're right," agreed Noah.

As the discussion continued, they realized that neither party was being difficult on purpose. They came to understand how different styles lead to different, often contrasting behaviors. Neither roommate was behaving *against* the other. Rather, each was simply doing what was natural to his style. By understanding *DISC*, potentially annoying behaviors could now be anticipated and adjusted so that neither would antagonize the other.

Although not all disagreements between roommates are driven by *DISC* styles differences, an understanding of the styles can help minimize, and in some cases, prevent conflict from occurring.

THE SCHOOL/LIFE BALANCING ACT

Many of today's students, whether they're taking courses online or attending a brick-and-mortar school, juggle much more than just homework assignments and getting to classes on time. An individual's *DISC* style can drive how one seeks to create balance between school and the other elements of life is. Sometimes, we get so caught up in our own style-driven approach, we fail to tap into the full range of strategies that will help create balance.

Example: Abby is a 25-year-old single parent with a five-year-old son. Each morning, she leaves him at a daycare center while she works in the city as a part-time receptionist. In the evening, Abby attends a community college.

While meeting the demands of her schedule and commitments is daunting enough, the prospect of taking on an even heavier education workload down the road has left Abby feeling overwhelmed. Abby is a *Cs* combination.

During her lunch break, Abby often dines with her friend, Mei, in a downtown cafeteria. Mei is a second-generation immigrant, and her strong *D* style drives her desire to achieve. She takes only a class or two each semester so she can chisel her way to a degree while working a full-time shift at a clothing store in a local mall, and another half-shift at night cleaning office buildings with a crew from a maintenance company.

"You're not looking so happy today," said Mei. "Is something wrong?"

Abby paused, and then decided to just let it out. "I don't know. I just feel like I'm not doing anything right. My son is upset with me for being in daycare so much. I stay up too late with him to compensate, but then he's a mess the next day and the daycare complains about his tantrums.

All of this leaves me wiped out for work and school."

"You want to know what I think?" asserted Mei.

Abby smiled, "Do I have a choice?"

"You can't just run around trying to please everyone else at your own expense. You'll end up both physically and emotionally drained," said Mei.

"Too late," said Abby.

"You need to prioritize," said Mei. "I know your son is only five, but you need to explain the situation in language he can understand. End the mommy-guilt and get the kid to bed. You need to be at your best, and running around without sleep is not good for either of you. Next, carve out an hour, say from 7 to 8 A.M., for yourself. Use it anyway you like—for school, to read a good book, to go for a walk. Make time for you, and then keep prioritizing everything else that needs to happen in the course of the day."

"Just like that? You make it sound so easy," sighed Abby.

"Well, it *is* simple, if you decide to make it simple," declared Mei. "You put too much pressure on yourself to be perfect at everything. Maybe good enough needs to be good enough at this point in your life. What's your alternative? Complain to me next week about being burned out?"

"I know you're right, but that's just not me," said Abby.

"I understand, but you're taking care of everyone but yourself," explained Mei. "Is that a good thing?"

"I guess not," said Abby. "But you're able to handle school and work because you accept that everything doesn't have to be perfect."

"Exactly!" exclaimed Mei. "What's the worst thing that can happen? Is your son going to grow up hating you? Are you going to get fired and fail out of school?"

Abby smiled. "That'll be difficult, but I can see that it would take the pressure off if I change my approach. I'll give it a try."

In this scenario, Abby was locked into her own *Cs* style. By utilizing Mei's *D* style approach, she gained an alternative way to handle her situation.

Each style has strengths and challenges when it comes to balancing the multiple commitments of school and life. Here's a look at how each style may deal with this issue:

D's tend to have a conquering mentality whereby they start with big priorities and work their way through lesser tasks as needed. However, *D*'s can overlook the impact their decisions have on others, so they need to stay conscious of the details that impact the results they seek.

The *I*'s optimistic mindset sometimes inspires them to take on too much, but their belief in themselves can drive their ability to make things happen. The challenge for the *I*'s is to make sure that they plan ahead and don't wait until the last minute to finish school projects.

The methodical nature of *S*'s keeps them organized, but they can easily overburden themselves by trying to keep everyone happy while they work to achieve their own goals.

The *C*'s ability to create plans and then focus on the details can help them to work within an established structure to balance school and life. But when the unexpected happens, they can get thrown off kilter.

Understanding the strengths and challenges of each style enables each person to accentuate their natural strengths while also developing skills from other styles. It simply means that individuals can intentionally choose behaviors that are not as natural but are needed for the situation at hand. *DISC*-inspired self-awareness increases your menu of options for handling just about any situation.

CHOOSING A MAJOR

Although improving self-awareness is important at any stage in life, college-age young adults are at a significant decision point. The subject they choose to major in will determine the initial trajectory of their careers. They want to select a path that they will enjoy and at the same time, they hope that all of their hard work will land them a financially rewarding job. No pressure.

Understanding one's strengths and challenges from a *DISC* style perspective can be a valuable starting point for exploring career options.

Example: Sean hurried out of class late for his meeting. "Not good," he thought to himself and then reflected, "I've got three years of college left. Why am I meeting with a career counselor now?"

Arriving at the counselor's office out of breath and dripping with sweat, Sean took his seat, resigned to wasting the next hour.

"You're late," she said.

"Yeah, sorry about that." Changing the subject quickly, he pointed to a foot-tall rocket on her desk. "Hey, that's really cool."

"My 10 year old made it," replied the counselor, handing it over to Sean. "He's crazy about Space."

Examining the rocket, he replied, "Me, too."

"So tell me Sean," the counselor began, "have you started to think about what you want to major in and what you might want to do after you graduate?"

"I'm not sure," shrugged Sean. "I've been thinking about something in engineering."

"OK," she nodded. "Why's that?

"Engineers seem to do well. And that's what my dad does."

"Has your father talked to you about his job?" she continued.

"A little bit. He helps design huge energy plants. He gave me a tour last year of a new one they're building. It's awesome."

"That *does* sound interesting. Tell me, are you a lot like your dad?" asked the counselor.

"What do you mean?"

"I mean your interests and your hobbies. Do you like the same things, have the same skills?"

"Well, he's more organized than I am. He's big on planning everything. I'm more spontaneous. I just like to go for it and see what happens."

The counselor smiled. "That's an interesting observation, Sean. I'd like to show you something. Here's that *DISC* profile I asked you fill out online last week," handing Sean his profile report. "Take a moment to read through it."

Within moments, Sean's jaw dropped as he gazed with wide eyes at the description of his style. "This totally pegged me," he stated.

"How so?" asked the counselor.

"Well, I do get excited about big ideas and cool technology—like the energy plant. I'm definitely outgoing and I love a good adventure. It says people like me are multitaskers. That's so true! My girlfriend is amazed at how I jump from one thing to the next, manage to get everything done, and still find a way to have fun with my friends. My grades are as good as hers, but she's so disciplined about studying. I guess that's why my dad likes her so much!"

"Sean," the counselor replied, "I'm going to play devil's advocate with you for a moment. Doesn't engineering require intense focus, staying within pre-defined systems and processes, and paying close attention to the details?"

"I guess so," Sean replied. "But those energy plants are incredible! I really think that I'd enjoy working there."

"It's exciting to be part of something large and impactful," replied the counselor. "But what about the actual job, 9 to 5, day after day, year after year? Have you thought about the daily responsibilities of being an engineer?"

"Not really," Sean acknowledged. "Do you think it's not a good fit for me?"

"That's for you to decide, Sean," the counselor said with a smile. "I'm just asking you to think about how *you* are wired, not your father. I'd suggest that you research what the daily realities of the job would be. Maybe you'll choose to be an engineer, perhaps you'll choose something else. But if you carefully consider what makes you tick and then align those attributes with a well-researched career choice, you might not consider your job 'work' at all. It will be a natural extension of who you are, and that's a really fun way to make a living."

"That makes sense," said Sean, "So based upon my style, what kind of jobs are a good match for me?"

The counselor smiled. "Let's explore that together."

For anyone who is at a turning point in their career, whether it's at the beginning, as in Sean's case, or at a mid-course correction, a careful examination of one's style-driven needs can lead to smart career choices. All too often, individuals choose jobs that do not fit their personalities. When this happens, work becomes drudgery and is reduced to a means to earning a paycheck so that life can be enjoyed *outside* of the workplace. However, as Confucius noted, "If you enjoy your job, you don't have to work a day in your life."

DISC AND YOUR TEACHER

Every student knows that a teacher can make or break a course. With the right instructor, the material comes alive and feeds the learner's passion to acquire more knowledge. By contrast, when a student's learning style is at odds with an instructor's teaching methodology, the subject matter itself becomes much less appealing.

DISC-savvy students realize that their teacher's behavioral style may well drive the way he or she teaches the class. This insight enables students to separate out the content of the material from the teaching style of the instructor.

Example: Emma and Olivia sat down for coffee in between classes. Olivia was in a good mood. Emma was not.

"That was a great class," said Olivia.

Emma's eyes grew large, "You think so? I find our teacher to be so...combative. Assigning us to debate teams on the first day? Most of us don't even know each other, and we haven't even covered the basics yet."

"But that's what made the class interesting," replied Olivia.

"I'm taking Poly Sci to learn about our political system, not get into an argument on day one," said Emma.

"We weren't arguing," responded Olivia with a laugh. "It was an exchange of views. It gave everyone the opportunity to put their perspectives out there."

"Not for me," Emma sighed. "I didn't say a word."

"Well, you could have. It's not the teacher's fault that you didn't participate."

Taken aback, Emma said nothing.

Olivia suddenly realized that this conversation wasn't light banter to Emma. Choosing her words more carefully, she said, "I didn't mean to offend you. I just see debates as a way of getting people to think about their beliefs and then trying to influence others. I get that you don't like to do that. I just don't understand why."

Emma took a moment to consider her reply. "Not everyone thinks on their feet so quickly," she replied. "My opinions are not so strong that I want to just yell them across the room. That doesn't help anyone. Honestly, I'm feeling like I should drop this course and find something else."

An instructor's behavioral style is critical to the focus, pace, and experience of a course. Olivia, a *D*, experienced a lively exchange that ignited her own passion for the subject. Emma, an *S*, found herself put off by what she perceived to be a conflict. However, if she were to drop out of the course, she would miss significant opportunities for growth.

In terms of skills, Emma's inclusive nature could have been critical to bridging differences and forging consensus within the larger group. By occasionally stepping out of her comfort zone to speak up, she might have been surprised at how much weight her opinions carry.

Since *S*'s do not often speak with conviction, when they do assert themselves, people stop and listen. Emma may also have discovered that by practicing behaviors that are not natural, she would have stretched herself to learn new skills. In the workplace, these skills might help her to be more successful in influencing others.

From a larger perspective, when a student's style is opposite from a teacher's approach, they can mistakenly reject the course, when really they are merely rejecting the teacher's methodology. By understanding the styles, students can make better decisions about choosing a field of study and a career.

MAKING THE GRADE WITH
GROUP PROJECTS

In school, as in the workplace, people are often grouped into teams for specific assignments. In many cases, these groups run into difficulty, not because of lack of skill, knowledge, or motivation, but rather due to the style makeup of its members.

Example: It was the first day of classes at a local college. Sophomores Brianna, Miles, Kayla, and Julian were randomly assigned to work on a major project for a business class. As their first meeting opened, Brianna immediately made it clear that she "knew" exactly what their first priority should be. She cut through the pleasantries and pointed at a specific section of the assignment sheet, as if she had written it and declared, "This is what we need to do first. Everyone agree?"

Miles interrupted, "But that's the biggest, most challenging section." Pointing to a different part of the project, he continued, "Why don't we start here? It's easy and it'll get us moving and excited. Then we can tackle the big stuff."

Kayla looked puzzled and stated, "I don't understand. You both just randomly picked a place to start. What we need is a plan. Before we do anything, we should map out the entire project and then we can assign roles and create a timeline."

Julian patiently watched the discussion unfold and then said, "Let's all just relax for a minute. We're not going to get anything done by arguing. We need to work together if we're going to get a good grade."

Understanding the *DISC* styles clarifies how different styles prioritize. And these priorities drive how we organize our work.

As a *D*, Brianna didn't hesitate to attack the biggest challenge. What better way to make real headway toward meeting the team's ultimate objective?

Miles, fueled by his *I* enthusiasm, wanted to begin with the easiest element of the project in order to create momentum. This would energize the group and enable them to start off in a positive way.

Kayla's *C* style prioritized planning over action. Her need to organize the process allowed for the structure to ensure quality and follow-through.

Julian's *S* energy drove his desire for teamwork and cooperation. To him, building consensus through trust and respect was crucial for attaining success.

Style awareness can help students understand one another's approach without judging it as wrong or ineffective. This allows team members to capitalize on each other's strengths and minimize conflict as they work together.

So, for example, instead of Kayla saying, "You both just randomly picked a place to start," she could honor Brianna and Miles' approach by saying, "Those both sound like possible places to begin. Perhaps we can create a plan to make sure that we think it through before we get started."

The four *DISC* styles have four different approaches to tackling projects and each has merit. The challenge is to recognize one's own bias, appreciate contrasting perspectives, and choose the right one at the right time. All too often, people reject alternative approaches because they conflict with their nature. The simple shift from judging to valuing can make the difference between struggling to complete a project and working together cohesively.

SCHOOL STRESS

If there's one thing students can count on experiencing while they are at school, it's stress. And stress doesn't just impact physical and emotional well-being, it directly correlates to how successful a student will be at school. Those who understand how to manage their stress will be more focused and likely to earn better grades. Consider four people from four different walks of life with four different behavioral styles.

Example: Angela is a student working toward a Masters in Management degree. After 10 years of working in the food service industry, Angela sought to run her own fast-food franchise. Ambitious and capable, Angela was excited to take her career to the next level.

Working in project teams with fellow students, it didn't take long for Angela's team to recognize when she was under stress. Because *D*'s often set ambitious goals, circumstances that prevent progress or created ambiguity around the team's progress frustrated Angela. At times she became visibly agitated, as her tone became aggressive and even loud. While this initially put off her *S* and *C* teammates, they eventually realized that Angela was also very quick to let go of her stress and refocus on the next challenge, pushing the team in positive directions.

By the end of the semester, Angela realized that her desire to get things done quickly created stress for her team members, which ironically, slowed down their progress. She recognized that when running her own franchise, she would need to pay closer attention to how her behavior under stress impacted others.

Example: After two tours in Afghanistan, Carlos recently returned home to attend college. The shift from military to civilian life is dramatic and often causes stress that only fellow vets can truly appreciate. However, *DISC* is a tool that can be used with any population. As a C, Carlos tended to withdraw from his classmates when the stress of school and outside life weighed upon him. However, instead of slacking off under duress, he actually worked harder. A Biology major, Carlos' intensity to learn every formula and ace every lab experiment caught the eye of his instructor. When a project he was working on failed, the teacher took Carlos aside and congratulated him on his zeal for accumulating the most accurate data analysis. Carlos, however, was clearly unhappy.

Sensing that his stellar student was pushing a bit too hard, the teacher surprised Carlos by cracking jokes and ending with, "Look. You are clearly going to be successful in my class, but let's not get carried away. Mistakes are how we get better. And here, no will get hurt as a result, so feel free to lighten up at times."

Smiling, Carlos responded. "I guess I need to remind myself of that sometimes."

Introverted by nature, *C*'s tend to withdraw even further when under stress and typically work through difficult circumstances by analyzing the issues in the hopes of arriving at a logical solution. In overuse, this often leads to analysis paralysis. Stressed-out *C* styles ratchet up their intensity through hyper-focus and near-obsessive data analysis. In such situations, a touch of *I* energy can be helpful to deflect the harmful effects of stress.

Example: Tori is 23 and a single mom. She works in a department store in a local mall while balancing her schoolwork on a bachelor's degree through an online college. Although Tori was advised to take only two online courses given her work hours and family needs, her optimistic *I* style drove her belief that she could handle three.

At first, she completed each module on schedule. But as the semester continued, she fell further and further behind. Now, with just a week to go, there seemed to be more online classes to take than there was time to take them.

Tori's stress level went from not high enough to see a bad situation forming to being too high to solve the problem. She expressed her stress to coworkers, to friends, to her parents, to her neighbors, even to the cat. Fortunately, a C coworker came to the rescue by showing her how to use project-planning software to both better manage her time and help organize the many assignments and projects that were now competing for her attention. Gradually, her time management skills morphed from haphazard to the kind of methodical planning that would make a C or S proud. As her grades went up, her stress levels went down.

The stress that Tori experienced was driven by her approach to managing time. Like many I styles, Tori still has a few all-nighters in her near future, but this doesn't mean that she will do this throughout her career. Thanks to some helpful advice from a friendly C, Tori is on her way to adding excellent time management skills to her natural I gifts.

Example: Peng grew up in a remote region of China. He was a gifted child and his parents had been saving for the day that Peng would come to the United States to attend a college.

How could Peng's classmates tell he was under stress? They couldn't! Well, maybe that's overstating it a bit, but *S*'s are reluctant to reveal their true emotions when under stress. While Peng quickly made friends and found himself helping others with *their* stress, he was very reluctant to share his own anxiety about being a new immigrant halfway around the world from his family.

Peng's classmates assumed that Peng's quiet nature was culturally based and, thus, they were reluctant to "invade his space" by asking too many questions about his life in China. Ironically, as an *S* style, such genuine interest and sincerity was exactly what Peng needed to experience in order to trust others with his own issues.

Over time, Peng learned to be more assertive in class and with his friends, revealing how he felt about the issues that were important to him. He found that the more he shared, the easier it was to find common ground with others.

Managing stress is a key skill to getting the most out of any student experience. By understanding what causes stress and how you react to potentially stressful situations, students better channel their energies toward productive outcomes.

ACE THE INTERVIEW AND WIN THE JOB

Whether pursuing that coveted internship or job, interviews are often nerve-wracking rites of passage for both college students and recent graduates. And although the Internet is filled with sites that reveal the so-called "best" answers to common interview questions, using your own experiences via storytelling is often the most effective way to portray the unique value you would bring to an organization. Save the "I'm a hard worker" clichés for your competition.

However, if you're style is different from the interviewer, one of you will need to flex to the other person's style to create a strong connection…and the person doing the adapting should be *you*. So, when sharing stories, consider the style of the interviewer.

If, for example, the interviewer is a *D*, you may want to share a success story that starts with the results you delivered, and then back into the situation and actions you took. Beginning with the bottom-line captures a *D*'s interest and provides the framework for filling in the details. With *D*'s, brevity and clarity are your best bets toward making a positive impression.

When your interviewer is an *I*, feel free to smile and be more enthusiastic. *I*'s are drawn to positive energy. Share stories that emphasize your people skills and your ability to think out-of-the-box to solve problems. In addition, be excited about their company and prove it by discussing their products or services.

The *S* interviewer will most likely give you a warm, friendly vibe. However, do not mistake this for evidence that you've won the job. The *S* is simply treating you like a human being, not just an applicant. In this situation, your stories should focus on how your experiences have positively impacted other people, whether they are coworkers, customers, or the community. Excessive focus on efficiencies or profit may come across as cold to an *S*. This style is not just interested in what you do, but how you do it.

If you find yourself being interviewed by a C, patiently providing the details and logic behind your decision-making will impress. In this case, you can spend more time fleshing out the facts of your story. C's want to be sure that a new intern or employee will take diligent steps to ensure quality work, not be haphazard or allow excessive enthusiasm to result in sloppy mistakes. If you happen to have high *I* or *D* energy, you may want to tone that down in the presence of a *C* interviewer.

Your goal in an interview is not to answer questions, (after all, you are not under arrest), but to distinguish yourself from the competition, who are probably using the cliché's you have left behind. Combining effective storytelling with *DISC* awareness is a powerful strategy toward accomplishing this goal. Review the "People Reading" section in Part II to hone your skills in assessing the interviewer's *DISC* style through body language and tone. *DISC* is a powerful tool in the service of communicating your best self to others. Honor their style, and they will better appreciate how you can benefit their organization.

Postscript

B ack at Home, our bird friends gathered for breakfast at the dove family tree. Clark turned to Dorian and asked, "So, how did it go when you described the *DISC* styles to the eagle population?"

"I just focused on the bottom-line benefit, and it didn't take long for them to see its value," said Dorian.

"The owls were eager to explore every angle," said Crystal.

"In true form, they asked a lot questions," Clark added. "In fact, we have a few items to clarify with Xavier."

"If you can find him," said Indy with a grin.

"How about the doves?" Crystal asked Sarah.

"They were quiet for a while, so Samuel and I didn't know what to think. But later, we got great feedback that everyone took the styles to heart," Sarah said.

"Well, the parrots loved it!" Ivy volunteered. "We had a massive improv session, and each of us acted out a style. I got to play Dorian. It was hilarious!"

"And where, exactly, did this take place? Not at the Council Tree, right?" taunted Dorian.

"Uhhh...ummm..." said Ivy.

"Moving right along," smiled Clark, "has anyone spoken to Xavier?"

"I heard he was observing some humans camping just south of the Great Lake," Samuel answered. "Evidently, they were having some...*issues.*"

The birds all nodded.

Just a few feet from the group, a brownish-red figure slipped away unnoticed.

"Everyone has issues," thought Xavier, "but once people discover and embrace the styles, their lives will take flight in ways they could have never imagined."

With a flick of his tail, he was gone. There was still much work to be done....

Style Combinations

A s our friends realized at the fable's end, people can be a bit more complicated than birds when it comes to how they view and interact with the world. Our bird friends did not exhibit strong secondary styles, but most people do. In fact, you may have easily recognized yourself or others in two or more of the characters.

The secondary styles can play a decisive role in how we interpret and react to the people and situations around us. Perhaps you related most to Dorian's *D* style directness, but have a little bit of Indy's *I* playfulness. Or maybe you are most like Crystal's analytical *C* style with a touch of Sarah's empathetic *S* nature.

The following descriptions will help you to better understand the people in your life. Note that the primary style is denoted with a capital letter and secondary style is identified with a lowercase later. So, the examples above would be described as a *Di* and a *Cs*.

If you haven't gone to www.TakeFlightLearning.com
to take the free mini-assessment or upgrade to the
comprehensive "Taking Flight with DISC" report by
entering the code, *teachmemore*, you may want to do
that now. These reports will help you to understand
how the four styles combine to create your behavioral
style. The following descriptions will help you to better
understand others by considering both their primary
and secondary styles.

THE Di STYLE

Di's combine the decisiveness of the *Dominant* style
with the fun, social orientation of the *Interactive* style.
Di's demonstrate a strong desire to achieve results, but
they do so by embracing collaboration with others.
They are highly influential as they combine direct and
clear communication with high energy and enthusiasm.

In the workplace, *Di's* are visionary and drive organizational change. They take the lead and embrace risk-taking. *Di's* become frustrated in settings in which they must be passive followers of what is happening around them. *Di's* want to be engaged in creating the vision and executing big ideas, and often gravitate toward leadership roles. They thrive in settings where big ideas are embraced and don't get bogged down in over-analysis.

Di's tend to have a "ready-fire-aim" mentality and benefit a great deal from people who add structure to their world. Moreover, partnering with more detail-oriented people, such as *C's*, enables *Di's* to focus on their core strengths.

In overuse, *Di's* tend to lack patience, which can lead to impulsive decision making. Under stress, *Di's* become restless and externalize their stress, which can create anxiety in others.

THE Id STYLE

As one might imagine, *Id's* are similar in orientation to *Di's*. The difference is that when *I* is stronger than *D*, the individual is first and foremost a motivator. The *Id's* optimistic spirit drives people to action through boundless enthusiasm. They enjoy and even crave constant stimulation. *Id's* thrive in unstructured, free-flowing settings that encourage innovative approaches to achieve results.

Id's build morale in their work environment and generate excitement for goals and ideas. They intuitively sense people's moods and are effective at influencing others to get what they want. *Id's* enjoy forming strategic alliances that advance their ideas. However, their big-picture focus needs to be supported by others who are detail-oriented and think things through. *Id's* abhor negativity and skepticism. They have difficulty working with people so rigid or buried in the details of a project that they fear taking risks and thus miss the bigger picture.

In overuse, *Id's* externalize their stress, which can add frenzied energy to the environment. They can overuse their optimism, which can lead to unrealistic assessments of ideas and people. In a crisis, however, *Id's* are adept at mobilizing the troops for action.

THE Is STYLE

Is's are warm, sociable, and friendly. Their compassion for others enables them to quickly and easily build strong, lasting relationships. They are eager to lend a helping hand and are natural teachers and counselors. *Is's* display an interesting mix of self-confidence and modesty.

Is's are the voice of the people. They are empathetic and will not hesitate to advocate for those in need. *Is's* like to work in social environments in which they develop true friendships with their coworkers. They thrive in settings where people care about each other and enjoy personal connections beyond the work at hand.

Is's are less comfortable making difficult decisions that will negatively impact others. They also dislike working with aggressive people who do not respect the feelings of others.

Is's would be well-served to surround themselves with quality-focused people who provide structured processes. In addition, they may require others to take charge in high-pressure situations.

Under stress, *Is's* can become overly accommodating and neglect their own needs. With a natural tendency to assume the best in people, they can misread the intentions of others and be overly trusting. Their dislike of conflict can cause them to downplay issues that grow only worse over time, leaving them feeling hurt or betrayed when relationships turn sour.

THE Si STYLE

Like their close *Is* cousins, *Si's* are easygoing and relaxed, and they go with the flow. The key distinction, however, is that *Si's* focus on *others first,* then themselves. The *Supportive* style's empathic nature combined with the *Interactive* style's enthusiasm culminates in a "champion of the people" combination.

Si's strive to maintain harmony in relationships. They love to work in team settings and are committed to treating people with respect. *Si's* can be counted on to patiently lend an ear to someone in need. Their capacity for empathy without judgment easily attracts new friendships. While they typically avoid engaging in conflict, *Si's* are more than willing to mediate between others to restore peace.

Si's also add stability to professional environments by maintaining consistency through their methodical approach to completing tasks. Having built psychological safety around the status quo, *Si's* appreciate stable settings that feature long-term relationships and processes that do not require frequent and dramatic change.

Si's tend to overuse kindness, which can cause them to subjugate their own needs for the wants of others. Furthermore, given their sensitive nature, *Si's* can become easily offended and can even hold grudges for long periods of time. *Si's* internalize stress and can act passive-aggressively.

THE Cs STYLE

Logic and the need for accuracy drive the *Conscientious* style. After all, if it's not going to be done right, then why do it? The *C's* need for precision combined with the *S's* patience creates an individual with a strong quality focus. Essentially, *Cs's* are perfectionists.

Cs's think and plan ahead to avoid the unexpected. They make sure that ideas are carefully vetted by questioning assumptions, exploring alternatives, and considering worst-case scenarios. They thrive in settings in which they can receive and analyze tremendous amounts of information *before* reaching a conclusion or making a decision. Cs's like to work within clearly defined boundaries and desired outcomes, but enjoy overcoming challenges through intense focus and persistence.

Cs's need others who can see the big picture without getting bogged down in the details. Given their task-focused nature, Cs's can also benefit from people who add positive energy to the environment, boosting morale and providing encouraging feedback.

Cs's dislike working in settings that lack standard operating procedures. They are uncomfortable with sudden changes and loathe reckless risk-taking. The Cs's fear of making a mistake can lead to time-consuming processes that strive for error-free outcomes.

In overuse, *Cs's* can get so engrossed in their work that they may lose sight of the need to celebrate accomplishments and provide positive feedback to others. Under pressure, *Cs's* can get caught up in "analysis paralysis" and create perfect plans, but remain fearful of taking action.

THE Sc STYLE

Sc's naturally construct patterns that govern their world. This manifests in intense loyalty to people, brands, and procedures that have been proven successful over time. *Sc's* build psychological safety around the status quo by establishing consistency in everything they do. They prefer predictability over rapid innovation and calm environments over fast-paced ones. As a result, *Sc's* can get trapped in existing methodologies when new approaches might better capitalize on emerging opportunities.

Sc's are modest about their abilities. While this can be an endearing trait in personal relationships, such humbleness can come across as meekness to more assertive styles. Their aversion to candor and constructive conflict can lead to passive-aggressive behaviors that prolong and intensify issues instead of solving them.

Sc's shine in roles that demand both empathy and a curiosity for understanding why or how things have occurred. This allows them to be excellent listeners who can help *others* to work through issues. They avoid drawing attention to themselves and prefer quiet, intimate settings to large group gatherings. *Sc's* like people, but tend to have just a few very close friends. They lead rich inner lives and often have more ideas than they actually express.

Sc's dislike fast-paced environments with rapid shifts in priorities. They are planners who don't want to be surprised. *Sc's* don't like to say no—a trait that often leads to becoming overburdened with work, as they value both their commitment to the team and to quality results.

THE Dc STYLE

Dc's seek to get things done with both urgency and complete accuracy. They have high expectations of themselves and others. The *Dominant* style is driven to achieve big goals while the *Conscientious* style insists that every step be well planned and properly executed. While the *D* loves to visualize the big picture and set broad goals that advance the cause, the *C* side of the same person will delve into the details, slowing down the urge to take big leaps. This internal struggle creates the constant push and pull between the desire for results and the desire for quality. *Dc's* often believe that others will not strike the correct balance, and thus overburden themselves with work that could otherwise be delegated.

Dc's thrive in environments where they have great autonomy to both set the agenda and help ensure that processes are followed through accurately. Although *Dc's* provide great contributions to projects large and small, they need people to help them appreciate the emotional or psychological impact that decisions might have on others. *Dc's* are wired for task completion and goal acquisition, not nuanced communication skills or intuition about how people feel.

Dc's are highly efficient and don't like it when others lack a sense of urgency for accomplishing goals and maintaining accuracy. They view work as the place to make things happen, not to engage in social or emotional commitments.

In overuse, *Dc's* can become too demanding of both themselves and those around them. Left unchecked, their combination of *D*-inspired bluntness and *C*-oriented pickiness can add significant stress to the workplace.

THE Cd STYLE

Like the *Dc,* *Cd's* focus on both accuracy and tangible outcomes. Their stronger *C* nature, however, brings diplomacy and patience to their *D* drive for accomplishment. *Cd's* enjoy creating systems that will withstand rigorous quality standards while delivering significant results. They are talented planners but may overlook the human element that drives collaboration. *Cd's* speak in specifics, preferring facts and examples over emotion and intuition to build their case. With their methodical nature and tendency to explore every option before arriving at a decision, *Cd's* are often reluctant to make big, consequential decisions.

Cd's tend to have a formal demeanor, display a limited range of facial expressions, and either avoid or minimize physical contact. In overuse, *Cd's* can come across as cold, blunt, and detached in personal relationships. They are reluctant to discuss their feelings and tend to have a small, close circle of confidants.

THE DS/SD STYLE IN WHICH THE D AND S ARE RELATIVELY EQUAL

The *DS/SD* is one of the least prevalent styles. While their *D* nature focuses on results, their *S* nature cares about fairness and respect. This makes the *DS/SD* perfectly suited to fight for justice and equality. With tenacity and compassion, the *DS/SD* speaks up for those who are unwilling or unable. They are motivated by deeply held commitments and pursue their goals with persistence and devotion.

With the willpower of the *D* and the patience of the *S*, this style combination displays unwavering determination for their cause and have a strong sense of personal accountability.

While *DS/SD*'s can sometimes appear to be detached from others, they are actually deeply emotional people. They are sensitive and can be easily offended, though they may camouflage it well.

It can be difficult to predict the reactions of *DS/SD* people, as sometimes they're in *D* mode—direct and results-oriented—and at other times, they're in *S* mode—caring and accommodating. They can be highly independent or may want to be a part of team striving to achieve their objectives. Regardless, *DS/SD*'s are fiercely loyal to the people in their lives.

THE IC/CI STYLE IN WHICH THE I AND C ARE RELATIVELY EQUAL

IC/CI is also a rare combination of styles within an individual. These combinations are superb at perceiving both the big picture and the details of complex projects. By recognizing interconnected systems, *IC/CI*'s can link insights from one area to another and can predict the likelihood of success of a new endeavor very quickly.

Often it seems as though *IC/CI's* are painstakingly gathering tremendous amounts of data, while in other situations they seem to make snap judgments in rapid succession. This is because their voluminous *C* data is first stored and then accessed subconsciously through pattern recognition, culminating in what appears to be a flash moment of insight. However, because they quickly intuit solutions, *IC/CI's* can appear to be impulsive.

C's understand conventional wisdom. *I's* are willing to buck it. When you combine these traits, you get someone who has a thorough understanding of the past and a visionary picture of the future. This yields a resourceful innovator.

They tend to be strong communicators, as *C's* measure their words carefully and *I's* are naturally skilled at influencing others. *IC/CI's* have to balance their social needs with their solitary needs. They love to be in groups, but must recharge their batteries alone. Their solitary "downtime" is often when they are most creative.

ALL FOUR STYLES ARE
RELATIVELY EQUAL

Your style is characterized by equal strengths from all four styles. This means that no one style stands out as the predominant style. Typically there are two main drivers of this result: Either you display a significant amount of flexibility and adaptability, or you are experiencing a major, often difficult, change in your life.

If your life is fairly stable, you likely have the capacity to adapt to situations as needed. For example, if you need to be a direct, results-driven eagle or a high-energy, optimistic parrot, you can ramp up your energy. When you need to tone it down a bit and listen with dove-like empathy or the moment calls for focused attention with an owl's eye for detail, you can adjust accordingly.

The strength of this style, therefore, lies in its flexibility. However, there are two main challenges. First, others cannot predict how you will respond to a given stimulus. Will you be excited or calm, outgoing or soft-spoken, task-focused or people-oriented? Your unpredictability can leave others uncertain about how best to communicate with you. Second, because you can relate to every dimension of a situation, you may struggle with indecisiveness.

The other possible driver of this style pattern is that you are experiencing transitional change or upheaval in your life. Perhaps it's a new job or a change in your relationship status. Maybe you just moved or had a child. These major life events can cause us to rethink how we need to act. These changes bring out new behaviors or suppress long-established patterns. In turn, no single style dominates the others. When this occurs, usually after the changes settle down, your style will return to its previous state and one or two of the styles will take precedence over the others.